D0429239

WISDOM
FROM
WOMEN IN
THE BIBLE

Books by Dr. John C. Maxwell
Can Teach You How to Be a REAL Success

Relationships

25 Ways to Win with People

Becoming a Person of Influence

Encouragement Changes Everything

Ethics 101

Everyone Communicates, Few Connect

The Power of Partnership

Relationships 101

Winning with People

Equipping

The 15 Invaluable Laws of Growth

The 17 Essential Qualities of a Team Player

The 17 Indisputable Laws of Teamwork

Developing the Leaders Around You

How Successful People Grow

Equipping 101

Make Today Count

Mentoring 101

My Dream Map

Partners in Prayer

Put Your Dream to the Test

Running with the Giants

Talent Is Never Enough

Today Matters

Your Road Map for Success

Attitude

Attitude 101

The Difference Maker

Failing Forward

How Successful People Think

How Successful People Win

Sometimes You Win, Sometimes You Learn

Sometimes You Win, Sometimes You Learn for Kids

Sometimes You Win, Sometimes You Learn for Teens

Success 101

Thinking for a Change

The Winning Attitude

Leadership

The 21 Irrefutable Laws of Leadership

The 21 Indispensable Qualities of a Leader

The 21 Most Powerful Minutes in a Leader's Day

The 360 Degree Leader

Developing the Leader Within You

The 5 Levels of Leadership

Go for Gold

Good Leaders Ask Great Questions

How Successful People Lead

Jumpstart Your Leadership

Leadership 101

The Leadership Handbook

Leadership Promises for Every Day

Learning from the Giants

WISDOM FROM WOMEN IN THE BIBLE

GIANTS OF THE FAITH SPEAK INTO OUR LIVES

JOHN C. MAXWELL

NEW YORK BOSTON NASHVILLE

FaithWords
Hachette Book Group
1290 Avenue of the Americas
New York, NY 10104

www.faithwords.com

Printed in the United States of America

RRD-C

First Edition: March 2015
10 9 8 7 6 5 4 3 2 1

FaithWords is a division of Hachette Book Group, Inc.
The FaithWords name and logo are trademarks of Hachette Book Group, Inc.

The Hachette Speakers Bureau provides a wide range of authors for
speaking events. To find out more, go to www.hachettespeakersbureau.com
or call (866) 376-6591.

The publisher is not responsible for websites (or their content) that are not
owned by the publisher.

Library of Congress Cataloging-in-Publication Data

Maxwell, John C., 1947–
    Wisdom from women in the Bible : giants of the faith speak into our lives /
John C. Maxwell. — First [edition].
        pages cm
    Includes bibliographical references.
    ISBN 978-1-4555-5708-0 (hardcover) — ISBN 978-1-4555-8952-4
(large-print hardcover) — ISBN 978-1-4789-0332-1 (audio download) —
ISBN 978-1-4789-0331-4 (audiobook) — ISBN 978-1-4555-5709-7 (ebook)
    1. Women in the Bible.   2. Christian life—Biblical teaching.
3. Bible.—Biography.   I. Title.
    BS575.M369 2015
    220.9'2082—dc23
                                                              2014048812

To my wonderful mother, Laura Maxwell
(February 3, 1921–July 15, 2009):

Your unconditional love made me secure,
Your heartfelt prayers helped keep me safe,
Your wise teaching ushered in my faith,
Your patient listening made me feel understood,
Your steady example inspired me to become more,
Your lived-out faith inspired this book.

I miss you every day and look forward to
being with you again in heaven.

CONTENTS

ACKNOWLEDGMENTS

I'd like to say thank you to:

Charlie Wetzel, my writer;

Audrey Moralez, who contributed ideas and gave her perspective as a woman;

Stephanie Wetzel, who reviewed and edited the manuscript; and

Linda Eggers, my executive assistant.

WISDOM FROM WOMEN IN THE BIBLE

PREFACE

In 2010 I got the opportunity to speak at Joyce Meyer's Love Life Women's Conference. Joyce and I are good friends, and I've often appeared on her television show. On this day I chose to talk about how to live a fulfilling life, and about the importance of attitude. When I got up to speak, I told the audience that for ten years I had spoken to men at Promise Keepers events, but that I was glad that God had finally given me a *greater* audience to speak to. The whole place went nuts, and we had a wonderful time that day.

When I finished speaking, I couldn't help thinking about my mother, Laura, whom I'd lost the year before. No person has had a greater impact on my life. Mom taught me true love and modeled God to me every day. It didn't matter if I was dealing with a scraped knee, a bruised ego, or a broken heart: she was always there to give a hug, share a tear, and provide a listening ear. I learned love and respect from her. I cannot put into words what I gained from her wisdom and her unconditional love. Every day I miss her. But I take comfort in knowing that she lived a full life for eighty-eight years, and that she is now with the one she loves most: Jesus.

My appreciation for Mom got me thinking about all the influential women who have shaped who I am, taught me spiritual lessons, modeled leadership, and made my life meaningful. It all started with Grandma Minton, who interceded for me when I was a very young child. I can tell you, I was a very ornery child, so I really needed people to talk to God on my behalf. I believe she almost single-handedly prayed me into the Kingdom.

And then there was Miss Tacey, my fourth-grade teacher. I deserved a permanent spot in the cloakroom for the way I acted in class, but instead she gave me a permanent spot in her heart. She used to write me encouraging notes. Even today she still writes to me. When I publish a new book, she writes me a note to tell me how much she likes it. Recently she wrote one that said, "I had no idea you would turn out this way." Neither did I.

My sister-in-law Anita has also been a great influence. She, my brother Larry, my wife, Margaret, and I have traveled the world together. Anita has always been sunshine to my soul. Her beautiful spirit shines on every person she meets and lights up every situation she encounters.

I spent a lot of time with my younger sister Trish. She was called Patty back when we were kids. She loved to tag along with my brother Larry and me. Believe it or not, when I needed to buy my first car after I graduated from college, she was the one who lent me the money for the down payment. Trish and her husband, Steve, have two beautiful daughters. When Rachael was young, I called her Angel because of the angelic expression she always had. I called Jennifer Sweet Pea, which she loved.

Of course there is Margaret, the love of my life. I fell in love with her at camp when I was in junior high school. The moment I first saw her I knew she was the one for me. Including our dating years, we've been together for over fifty years! Her love for God and family has been a great blessing to us. Her years of faithful ministry have been a blessing to many.

Our whole world changed when our daughter, Elizabeth, arrived in our lives. I call her Apple of My Eye. Daughters always have a special place in a father's heart. Elizabeth has one in mine. And when our son, Joel, got married, Lis, our daughter-in-law, became a beautiful part of our family. Lis has been a delight, and she's made our son a better person.

Elizabeth and Lis have also done the most wonderful thing a human being can do for another person: they've given us grandchildren. Of course we have a special love for our grandsons, John and James. But Madeline, Hannah, and Ella are the three smartest, most talented, and most beautiful girls on the planet. All five of these children bring light into our lives.

Margaret and I just took Maddie and Hannah on a trip to Pennsylvania to celebrate their thirteenth birthdays. We filled them up with history at Gettysburg and in Philadelphia until they couldn't take any more. We had to take them to Hershey for the rides and the water park so that they could enjoy being kids again.

I have also been influenced greatly by the women whose stories are told in the Bible. From the time I was a child, Mom talked to me about these giants of the faith, people such as Ruth and Hannah, Abigail and Mary. The traits they modeled and the leadership they exhibited have provided invaluable lessons to me.

And that got me to thinking. What if I could write another *Giants* book focused entirely on the women whose stories have been so valuable to me? I imagined what it would be like to visit heaven for a day, see my mom again, and be introduced to these amazing women of the faith.

If you've read *Running with the Giants* or *Learning from the Giants*, you have an idea about what's coming. We will imagine what it would be like to spend time with nine giants of the faith. We'll walk with them, listen as they share wisdom from their lives, and take away lessons that can help us every day. In addition, I've asked nine important women in my life to share their perspectives in sections called "Woman to Woman." You'll hear from my wife, Margaret, my sister, Trish, Trish's adult daughters, Rachael and Jennifer, my brother Larry's wife, Anita, my daughter, Elizabeth, my daughter-in-law, Lis, and my two older granddaughters, Maddie and Hannah, who are thirteen. You don't have to be a woman to benefit from the lessons these women have to teach us. The truths they teach are universal.

So come along and join me as we take a journey and gain wisdom while walking with these giants of the faith.

RUTH

Follow Your Heart to Find Your Hope

I got up before dawn this morning. That's not uncommon. Decades ago I made a commitment to get up anytime I felt that God was waking me, even if it was in the middle of the night. I know it's God if I wake up with a compelling idea or with an urgent sense that I need to pray about something. When that happens I usually just slip out of my bedroom quietly to keep from waking Margaret.

That's what I did this morning. It's five o'clock and it's still dark outside. I'm now in my study, sitting in my favorite thinking chair. The pull of God was especially strong this morning, and I have a profound sense of anticipation, but I'm not sure what God is up to or what He has in store for me. I ask God to speak to me and to direct me in prayer. I close my eyes, and I wait.

A Vision

I try not to get distracted by thinking about my heavy travel schedule or the work that sits waiting for me on my desk. I want to quiet my mind and be open to whatever God has to say. For some reason my mind keeps shifting toward my mother. That's bittersweet. Any time I think about my mom I smile, because her love for me was unconditional. But it also makes me sad to think about her because she died in 2009. I still miss her.

Suddenly my head starts to swim. I want to open my eyes, but I can't. There are flashes of light like I'm seeing stars. And my ears start ringing. The next minute I have that feeling of falling you get sometimes when you're nodding off, and my body jerks. *Am I falling asleep?* I wonder.

When I open my eyes, I'm standing in a beautiful meadow filled with pink flowers on a sunny day. I can smell the grass and the pleasantly sweet scent of the flowers. I take a deep breath. The air is fresh and warm and dry.

I start to look around to take everything in, and that's when I notice you standing right beside me. You look as surprised as I feel. It's reassuring to know that I'm not alone in this experience.

The moment I am about to ask you how you got here, I hear a voice calling.

"John."

The sound almost makes my knees buckle, because the voice can belong to only one person: my mom.

I turn around and there she is, standing before me. I start to weep uncontrollably. I grab her in my arms, and then I bury my face in her shoulder as I did when I was a child.

When I pull my face up, she is smiling at me. She is as calm and steady and accepting as ever. Her face is youthful, and she doesn't seem to have a care in the world.

"Oh, John, it's so good to see you. I've missed being with you," she says. "I see you've brought someone with you. Good. You always did have a friend with you."

"Mom," I ask. "Are we—are we in heaven?"

"Of course, dear," she answers.

I gasp when I'm hit with an overwhelming thought, and I start to cry again. "Are we going to get to see Jesus?"

"No, John, I'm sorry, but we can't do that now. That will have to wait until your own time comes. But when it does, trust me. You won't be disappointed." Mom smiles. "Come along with me," she says as she walks across the meadow.

"Today we have a different purpose," Mom says. "You

and your friend are going to get to meet nine women—amazing women—each a giant of the faith. When you were a child, I taught you about each of them. But today you will meet them in person. And you will have an opportunity to learn from them about life and leadership. Their wisdom can help you greatly if you apply it to your life."

We haven't walked far when I see a woman in a robe that's the same pink color as the flowers in the meadow. Around her waist is a broad sash that has been embroidered with a pattern in gold thread. It reminds me of the stalks of wheat I saw in fields when I was a boy growing up in Ohio.

"Here is the first one," Mom says. A mischievous smile breaks over her face. "I won't tell you who she is. I'll let you figure that out on your own. Listen to what she has to say. She will guide you. And you'll see me again before you leave." With that, Mom turns and walks away.

"I greet you in the name of the Living God," the woman in pink says. "I have been asked to tell you my story. Walk with me." She walks slowly through the meadow. You and I move alongside her.

"When I married Mahlon," she begins, "I thought I was the most favored woman in the world."

The wife of Mahlon—this is Ruth!

"My father arranged the marriage, of course, and I

didn't even mind that Mahlon was not a Moabite like me," Ruth explains. "I also accepted that his widowed mother would be living in the same house with us. Mahlon was a good man. He was kind, hardworking—and handsome. I hoped for a good marriage. What I did not expect was to love this new family so deeply. As I got to know them, I came to love everything about them: their traditions and customs, and the God they worshipped wholeheartedly. They were my true family, more so even than my own mother and father, to whom I was born.

"We had been married only a short time, so short that God had not yet given us children, when the unthinkable happened. I lost my dear Mahlon. And before my mother-in-law, Naomi, and I were even finished mourning, Mahlon's brother, Kilion, also died. I understand that no one escapes pain or death in life, but this gutted me. Just when I'd found my right place, it was taken away from me. We were alone in the world, with no way to live. In those days a woman couldn't own property or direct her own affairs. She had to depend on a husband, brother, or father.

"Naomi insisted that Kilion's wife, Orpah, and I go back to our fathers' houses. We had been honorable women, so we knew they would take us back. Orpah left. But I—I felt like I had a huge decision to make. I felt like Naomi was my family. What was I going to do?

"What I decided that day taught me one of life's most important truths, and now I want to teach it to you." She stops walking, turns to face us, and says, *"Follow your heart to find your hope."*

Following Her Heart

Ruth pauses for a moment, watching us to see if we are listening carefully, taking in what she is trying to help us understand. Then she begins to walk again, with us at her side. And she starts to explain what she means:

"My Heart for Naomi Outweighed Everything Else"

"My decision was to stay with Naomi. Immediately we left Moab for Judah, her homeland. When we arrived in the town of Bethlehem, we had no hope. I could tell Naomi had given up. She thought God had abandoned her. I knew that she had come back home to die. So be it. If she was going to die, I would die with her. I would be buried alongside her, among her people, who were now my people. I didn't care what happened to me. My heart felt things my eyes could not see, and it knew what my mind could not understand. Naomi had been so good to me, how could I not be good to her?"

"My Heart for Naomi Led Me to Boaz"

"When we got to Naomi's old homeland, I knew I needed to do something so that we would not starve. God in His loving-kindness told His people to always leave the edges of the fields unharvested for people like Naomi and me. So I went to gather grain during the harvest.

"I believe it was no accident that I ended up in the fields of Boaz. When you make a God-honoring decision with the heart, God guides you with His hand. I didn't know it, but God had made a way for me. Boaz had already heard about me, and he protected me like I was a member of his household. He fed me and he even gave me extra grain to take back to Naomi."

"My Heart for Naomi Led Us to Hope"

"When Naomi found out I had spent the day in the fields of Boaz, her relative, she realized God was providing for us. It rekindled her hope and she came alive again. The old Naomi was back. She knew Boaz was a good man, so she told me what to do so that he would become our kinsman redeemer—and my husband. Where once all had looked dark and hopeless, we now possessed a bright future."

Life Lessons from Ruth

As we walk silently for a while, I think about what Ruth has told us. It must have taken a lot of courage for her to leave her home and everyone she knew to travel to an alien land. In that way, she was like Abraham. She would have been seen and treated like an alien—a foreigner. Despite this, she followed her heart.

When Ruth speaks again, it's as if she has anticipated my thinking. She says,

"Understand that in God's Eyes There Are No Outsiders"

"When we left for Judah, I knew I would be an outsider to the Children of Israel," says Ruth. "But I wasn't a foreigner to God. He accepted me as a part of His family. And He made it official when Boaz married me.

"Maybe you've felt like an outsider at times. Some people feel that way their whole lives, like they don't fit anywhere, like nobody understands them. Even Jesus was treated as an outsider. The people He came to save didn't recognize Him or want Him.[1] But you don't have to be on the outside looking in. God invites you to be a part of His family. All you have to do is say yes to Him, and you'll be His adopted child. He loves you and wants you."

"When You're in Distress, Let Love Motivate You to Change"

"My world fell apart when my husband, Mahlon, died. I had found my place in the world, and then it was taken away from me. What was I to do?

"What drives you when your situation is dire? Is it fear? Worry? Frustration? Resentment? Bitterness? None of those emotions will take you in the right direction. Instead look for love. Love will carry you forward. Follow your heart."

"Hold on to Faithfulness Because It Is the Father of Many Blessings"

"I trust God for Who He is, not for what He does. But God rewards faithfulness. I was faithful to Naomi, and God blessed me by directing me to Boaz. Boaz was faithful to God and His Law. When Boaz realized that we were relatives, and that someone in our clan needed to help us, he went to the elders of the town and contacted our nearest relative to see if he would help us. When that man couldn't fulfill his duty, Boaz took action to redeem our property and care for us. He was faithful to God, and as a result, God blessed both us and him.

"God always makes a way for those who love Him.

The guidelines He gave for the harvest blessed us with food.[2] The guidelines He gave for treating widows blessed us with a new family and me with a husband.[3] And of course, that led to my greatest joy of all, giving birth to my son Obed. He became a blessing as he fathered Jesse, who fathered David, Israel's great king and a man after God's own heart.

"When you are faithful to God, He will bless you. You may not know how He will do it or when He will do it, but you can always be sure that God is faithful."

The Prayer of Ruth

Ruth stops and says, "Before I leave you, I want to pray for you. Would that be all right?" We both nod yes.

"God My Redeemer,

"You are faithful and good. You love us and want the best for us. First I pray that my friends would know their own hearts. When they are in doubt or distress, help them to be sensitive to You. Speak to them through Your Spirit, and help them to have the courage to follow where You lead. And I pray that You would always reward them with hope. Amen."

When we open our eyes, we see that Ruth is smiling at us. "My friends," she says, "my time with you has come to an end. But your next mentor is waiting for you ahead, outside the gates of the city. Keep walking along this path, and you will find her." With that Ruth turns and walks back the way we came.

Leadership Lessons from Ruth

We hesitate a moment. Which do we want more? To stop Ruth and ask her questions? Or to move forward and meet the next person? We sense our time here is limited and decide to keep walking. As we do, I reflect on what Ruth said and on her story in the Bible. With each step, leadership lessons become clear to me from Ruth's life:

1. Do What You Know Is Right, Not What Looks Right to Others

The logical thing for Ruth to do when her husband died was to go home to her own family and look for a new husband. Naomi suggested she do that. And Ruth's sister-in-law Orpah followed that advice.

Ruth could have allowed her questions and doubt to influence her to leave Naomi. But instead her heart came to grips with what she believed. She moved from the agony of questions she could not answer to the reality of answers she could not escape. She felt a deep conviction that she was to stay with Naomi. And she followed that conviction.

As leaders we need to remember that. Strong convictions precede great actions. When we know something is right—and that conviction is bolstered by the knowledge that our motives are pure, as Ruth's were—we need to follow through. Others may second-guess our thinking and our decision-making. But when we know what's right, we can't let those things throw us off. We need to stand by our convictions. As Albert Mohler, president of the Southern Baptist Theological Seminary, said, "Convictions are not merely beliefs we hold; they are those beliefs that hold us in their grip."

2. Following Your Heart with Integrity Can Increase Your Influence with Others

Because Ruth followed her heart and went with Naomi to Bethlehem, her influence on others increased. Instead of looking down on her as a foreigner, the Hebrews noticed her and admired her. She gained the favor of Boaz, who told her, "I've heard all about you—heard about the way you treated your mother-in-law after the death of her husband, and how you left your father and mother and the land of your birth and have come to live among a bunch of total strangers. GOD reward you well for what you've done—and with a generous bonus besides from GOD, to whom you've come seeking protection under his wings."[4]

When Ruth followed her heart and made her decision, she stood out from the beige lives of others. She impressed the people of an entire town, including the elders, who blessed her, declaring,

> May GOD make this woman who is coming into your household like Rachel and Leah, the two women who built the family of Israel. May GOD make you a pillar in Ephrathah and famous in Bethlehem! With the children GOD gives you from this young woman, may your family rival the family of Perez, the son Tamar bore to Judah.[5]

By following her heart and doing what she knew was right, Ruth went from being a foreigner to being someone who was respected, blessed, and honored.

When you follow your heart and do the right thing,

your leadership potential increases. Leadership is influence, so anything that increases your influence and favor with others makes it easier for you to lead.

3. Remember to Be Humble and Keep Working as God Blesses You

When Boaz recognized Ruth and started to bless her, it might have been natural for her to slack off. After all, she was receiving the favor of a relative who had the power to redeem her and the property that had once belonged to Naomi's husband. But Ruth remained faithful and kept working hard. Scripture says she worked hard before Boaz invited her to eat with him. Afterward she got right back to work and gleaned in the field until evening. And then she threshed what she had gathered before going home. This is the pattern she followed until both the barley and wheat harvests were done.

When God grants you favor as a leader and you receive His blessings, don't let it go to your head and don't let up. Keep working. When you have favor and momentum, push ahead. Naomi understood this. When she and Ruth began to receive Boaz's favor, they didn't just sit back and enjoy the provisions he made sure they received. Naomi capitalized on them. She told Ruth to lie at Boaz's feet, as a sign of her desire to seek his protection.

And he graciously gave it. He immediately became their advocate.

God wants His people to be recognized by others because of their love. I think we too often forget that. Ruth's words of wisdom are a good reminder. If we love others and follow our heart in the way we treat everyone, it's hard to go wrong.

Woman to Woman

Whenever I hear the story of Ruth, I'm always struck by how she reacted to the loss of her husband and brother-in-law. She and Naomi suddenly found themselves alone in the world, at the end of their rope, with no way to change their circumstances. In their culture, without a man, they had almost no options. If anyone could have felt like a victim, Ruth could. And she could have easily given in to her grief and lost hope.

But Ruth didn't surrender to despair and hopelessness. Instead, after she and Naomi arrived in Bethlehem, she immediately went to work looking

(Continued)

for ways to provide for the two of them. The solution she found involved hard manual labor, but she didn't let that stop her. She worked all day, every day, picking up the scraps left over after the harvesters had done their work. She chose to do something, even when she didn't see where God was leading.

The lesson I learn from Ruth as a woman is that I don't ever need to see myself as a victim of circumstances. Especially in a modern world with many more options than Ruth had, I can instead choose to have hope and look for a way to overcome challenges. I don't have to be defined by what has happened to me. Rather I can follow God's lead and take action, and it will open the way to changing my circumstances and finding fulfillment and joy according to God's plan.

—Margaret Maxwell

Questions for Reflection or Discussion

To learn more about Ruth, read Ruth 1:1–4:22 and Matthew 1:5–6.

1. Whom do you relate to most in the story of Ruth: Naomi, Ruth, or Boaz? Explain.
2. What would you have done in the place of Naomi's daughters-in-law? Would you have gone home like Orpah? Or would you have followed Naomi to Bethlehem? Why?
3. When Ruth moved to Bethlehem with Naomi, she was in a pretty difficult situation where she had very little power to control her destiny. How does that kind of situation make you feel?
4. How much did Ruth rely on God and how much did she rely on her own initiative and ability to work hard?
5. How do you try to balance God-reliance and self-reliance when facing a difficult personal challenge?
6. Where or how do you find hope when life feels hopeless?
7. Where in your life would you currently benefit from following your heart more?

SARAH

*Don't Complicate God's Promise
with Your Solution*

We walk to the crest of a hill and before us is the most magnificent thing we've ever seen. It's a city, but it's like nothing any living person has ever seen. It reminds me of the ancient city of Jerusalem, except the walls are smooth and look like thick glass. The city is enormous. Rising above the walls are thousands of brightly colored buildings that glint in the light. A kind of glow seems to come from the heart of the city, even though it appears to be broad daylight.

Our pathway has become a paved street, and we see that it leads toward a circular opening in the city wall that has a large open gate. We keep walking toward it. While we are still some distance from the wall, both sides of our paved street become lined with low decorative walls. They seem to be made of the same kind of material as the city's walls. It looks like thick pieces of glass.

While we are still several hundred yards away from the gate, we notice a woman sitting on the wall. She is dressed in a long garment of yellow with a head covering of the same fabric. It's not until we get close to her that we can see her hair is gray and her face is gently wrinkled. She smiles at us, and we're struck by her beauty. She stands, and we see that she still has the figure of a woman in her prime.

"Ah, you've arrived," the woman says. "Sit with me so we can talk." She sits and we join her. The top of the low wall is perfectly smooth and very hard.

"When I was a girl, I believed I was going to have the most wonderful life. I married a man from a good family—from my own clan, in fact." She smiles. "Our future looked bright, and I planned to raise a large family with him.

"But a year passed and then another, and still I had no children. With each birthday I grew more anxious. Twenty-five. Thirty. Thirty-five. Forty. The time was slipping away. I was watching myself become an old woman. Forty-five. It was still possible. I had known women to have children in their forties. Then I turned fifty. Fifty-five. And I knew: my time to have children had passed. I mourned for five years. And then at age sixty, I let it go. What could I do? Old women don't bear children."

Could this be Sarah, we wonder?

God's Promise

"When I was sixty-five, God spoke to my husband, Abraham."

It *is* Sarah. She was there when it all began, when God made a covenant with a mere man and promised to bless the world through him. Sarah continues, "God promised that Abraham would become the father of a great nation. Do you know what that meant?" she asks. A dozen thoughts run through my mind. Which one might she mean? "It meant I would finally be blessed with children—enough children to start a nation. I would finally be blessed by God. I could hardly believe it. At a time when other women have grandchildren or great-grandchildren, I would finally become a mother.

"When Abraham told me God's promise meant great changes for us, I said yes:

"I said yes when Abraham asked me to leave my home.

"I said yes when Abraham asked me to accompany him on a thousand-mile journey to an unknown land.

"I said yes when Abraham asked me to live like a nomad in the wilderness.

"I even said yes when Abraham asked me to tell others I was his sister.

"I met each day with expectation. Would this be the day God would place a child in my womb?

"But the days turned into months, and the months years. I waited ten years, and still God did not fulfill His promise. And I couldn't see *how* He would do it. So I decided I needed to do *something*. I told Abraham to have a child with Hagar, the servant I had acquired when we were in Egypt."

Sarah stands up and faces us. We start to get up too, but she waves her hand, indicating that we should stay seated. "Have you ever felt like you needed to help God? So you took matters into your own hands?" She laughs. "Why do I even ask? Of course you have. Do you know anyone who hasn't? But really we should know better. I know better now, and I can confidently tell you this: *Don't complicate God's promise with your solution.*"

The Consequences of Sarah's Solution

"I thought I was helping God. All I was doing was making life worse for myself. The moment Hagar became pregnant, she despised me. She had something I didn't, and she felt she had the upper hand. When Ishmael was born, it didn't get any better. Every day I had to look at him and watch the way Abraham treated him. It planted a seed of bitterness in my heart.

"I blamed Hagar for the mockery of her son Ishmael.

"I blamed Abraham for the misery caused me by Hagar.

"I blamed God for not giving me a baby.

"But the reality is that I brought this trouble upon myself. God promised me *what*: He said I would have a son. He did not promise me *when*."

Life Lessons from Sarah

Sarah smiles as she thinks for a moment. Then she sits again where she can make eye contact with both of us, and she begins to speak:

"Don't Try to Get Ahead of God When He Isn't Moving Fast Enough for You"

"We always have an opinion about how God should do things. Usually we want what we want now. And our reasons seem so good to us. But no matter how strong, clever, resourceful, or strategic we are, we cannot out-think God, nor should we try to get ahead of Him.

"As I looked into my past, I could see God's hand in every step of Abraham's and my faith journey. But back then, when I looked toward the future, I could not. I felt uncertain then, but now I know: those who can see God's hand in their lives can put their lives in God's hands.

"God sees the entire universe. He wants the best for everyone at every time in human history. And He is weaving together the threads of everyone's lives. How can we possibly think we know better than He does?"

"Our Surrogate Solutions Are Always Poor Substitutes for God's Promises"

"When we try to create our own solutions, our actions always produce negative consequences. When I suggested that Abraham use Hagar as a surrogate for me, I turned a faithful servant into an enemy. My marriage became strained. My relationship with God was affected. And I caused a feud between the descendants of Isaac, the son I eventually had, and Ishmael, the son of Hagar. That conflict continues even to this day.

"There is probably something you want right now that

God has said He will give you. And you may be trying to figure out how to get it in your timing instead of God's. Don't do it. Even your best will never compare to what God has planned for you. God reveals things to us on a need-to-know basis. When you don't need to know, God does not reveal His will. In those times we must wait."

"When You Must Wait, Focus on God's Character, Not Your Circumstances"

"When God is silent and we are required to wait, we often turn our attention to the wrong things. We focus on our circumstances and see nothing but the obstacles. That's what happened to me. As time went by and my situation seemed more dire in my own eyes, I began to feel increasingly vulnerable.

"We need to remember that our circumstances—no matter how insurmountable the obstacles may seem—are nothing to God. His promises are true no matter what. Knowing God's will is not enough. Doing God's will is essential. That requires total trust."

"God's Miracles Happen Only When You're Faced with the Impossible"

"Only when we're in the place where we need the impossible is God able to perform a miracle. God loves to fulfill

His promises under such circumstances. God gave me the son He'd promised, Isaac, and He did it when I was ninety years old! Never forget that *nothing* is impossible for God, and miracles are everyday occurrences to Him.

"So if you're in a tough spot, you're uncomfortable, and the impossible is the only thing that can help you, then you are a candidate for a miracle. And if God has made you a promise, you can be sure He will fulfill it."

The Prayer of Sarah

Sarah smiles once more. She seems to suppress a bit of a chuckle. Scripture says that when God told her she would have a son in her old age, she laughed. I imagine it was with bitterness. Now she seems to smile and laugh with joy. She offers to pray for us.

"Sovereign Lord,

"I pray that in the future when a day comes that these people feel desperate and their circumstances look impossible to them, they will rely on You completely, and You will bless them for it. In such times, help them to remember Your promises, to wait with patient expectation, and to hold out for Your miracle. Amen."

When Sarah finishes praying, she smiles at us once again. "Go on into the city," she says. "The next person will be waiting for you just inside the walls." We walk forward, thinking about what she said. We look back once and see that she is watching us, and still she is smiling.

Leadership Lessons from Sarah

Sarah may not have influenced large numbers of people during her lifetime, but the influence she had shaped the world. And we can learn valuable leadership lessons from her:

1. Let Your Leadership Decisions Be Guided by Faith, Not Driven by Frustration or Fear

Someone once said that faith is what you have when you don't have all the facts but you have God. Sarah was married to a strong man of faith, yet she fed her doubts and frustrations. Certainly she had plenty of valid reasons for feeling frustrated. She had already suffered with not having children during the normal childbearing years. Then after receiving a promise from God that she would have a child, she had to wait an additional twenty-five years. I can't imagine being patient through such circumstances. But I also know God wants us to focus on our faith in Him.

There have been many times in my life as a leader when I've lost my patience and wanted to grab hold of a situation to change what was happening. Perhaps the greatest frustration I ever faced was when I was a senior pastor trying to lead Skyline Church through a transition to a new location. For more than a decade we faced obstacle after obstacle. There were many times when my frustration boiled over and I had to stop, talk to God about how I felt, and put my focus back on my faith in Him. It's easy to believe in God's blessings. It's sometimes harder to believe in His timing.

One of my mother's favorite verses, which she quoted often, was 1 Peter 5:7: "Leave all your worries with him, because he cares for you."[6] If you are frustrated in your leadership, don't let it provoke you into making bad decisions. Turn to God and allow Him to help you work through your emotions. And always remember the words of Charles Spurgeon: "God is too good to be unkind. He is too wise to be confused. If I cannot trace His hand, I can always trust His heart."

2. Never Use Your Influence to Manipulate People for Personal Gain

Sarah had great influence over two people in her life: her husband, Abraham, and her servant Hagar. When she could no longer stand the frustrations of her life, she used that influence over the two of them to lead them into a bad decision. That backfired on everyone.

Author and congressman Bruce Barton said, "Sometimes when I consider what tremendous consequences come from little things, I am tempted to think there are no little things." Just because we have power doesn't mean we should use it—especially if we are thinking of using it for our own benefit. It's easy to rationalize such decisions. But they almost always lead to regret.

3. Don't Blame Others for the Consequences of Your Bad Decisions

When Hagar became pregnant after Sarah told Abraham to sleep with her, their relationships turned sour. Hagar looked down on Sarah, and Sarah became abusive. Sarah knew she had made a bad decision, yet she blamed it on Abraham. She told him, "It's all your fault that I'm suffering this abuse. I put my maid in bed with you and the minute she knows she's pregnant, she treats me like I'm nothing. May GOD decide which of us is right."[7]

When we lead others, we are in a position to place the blame on others, and we can easily get away with it, because the people we lead are often reluctant to speak out against us. But good leaders don't do that. Instead they take less than their share of the credit and more than their share of the blame.

When you make poor decisions, don't try to cover them up or place the blame on someone else's shoulders. Take responsibility. God knows when we're in the right and when we're in the wrong. Allow Him to keep accounts and reward you accordingly.

As a person who has been impatient his entire life, I needed Sarah's words of advice. All too often I've tried to help God and offer Him my own solutions. I know better, but I still do it. We should always try to remember that even our very best cannot possibly compare to anything God has in mind.

Woman to Woman

When I think of Sarah, I am reminded that nothing is impossible for God. It is easy to say that I believe that God is a God of miracles, that nothing is too difficult for Him, but when my circumstances look impossible, I am forced to wrestle with this truth in the deepest corners of my heart.

(Continued)

Sometimes I do not understand God's ways or His timing in my life. When I try to "make sense" of it all, I simply cannot. It is in these moments that I am thankful for Sarah's story because I know that she could not make sense of God's plan either. I know this because she tried to substitute her own plan for God's promise, and I am often guilty of this same offense.

Despite Sarah's lack of faith, God was faithful. He did for Sarah as He had promised. When I am tempted to close my heart to God and rely on my own resources, I am reminded of His faithfulness. He is faithful even when I am faithless. And when I dare to open my heart to trust Him even when I cannot see the outcome, He gives me faith to rest in the promise that He is working ALL things together for my good and His glory.

—Rachael Watson

Questions for Reflection or Discussion

To learn more about Sarah, read Genesis 12:1–23:2.

1. How would you respond if your spouse told you he or she had heard from God and was asking you to move to an unknown land?

2. Do you think it was fair for Sarah to have to wait so long to have a child? Explain.

3. Why do you think God delayed the process for so long and made both Abraham and Sarah wait?

4. God changed the name of Abram, which means "exalted father," to Abraham, which means "father of many." Why do you think God changed Sarai's name to Sarah, when both names mean "princess"?

5. How do you usually deal with frustration in your life? Do you lash out, retreat and seethe, try to take control, or give up?

6. How do you think God wants you to react?

7. What disappointment are you currently dealing with? How might others be able to help you deal with it in a God-honoring way?

RAHAB

God's Story Is Full of Surprises

As we walk toward the gate, we start to get a sense of how tall the walls are and how huge the city must be. As we get closer, we're astounded by what we see. The material that makes up the gate is creamy white and shimmers. It looks like it's made out of pearl. Beside the gate stands a single guard who must be at least twelve feet tall! A sword is sheathed by his side. He watches stoically as people pass in and out of the city.

The people around us seem to be dressed in every kind of clothing from every nation and era in human history. I see people dressed in modern military uniforms, animal skins, togas, tribal regalia, European and Japanese armor, robes, breeches, long dresses, short dresses, and suits. Some people wear not much clothing at all. It's as though we're on the back lot of a movie studio and actors from a hundred different exotic movies mingle together. But these people are real, not costumed performers.

Before we pass under the arch of the gate, I notice a word in Hebrew written above the door: יְהוּדָה. I spent two years learning Hebrew to write one of my books, so I can decipher the meaning. It says "Judah."

We walk through the gate, which leads us into a long tunnel. The street is wide and the walls beside us, as well as the arched ceiling above us, are perfectly smooth—like glass. The tunnel is brightly lit, and when we get about one hundred feet inside, which seems to be the halfway point, I realize there are no artificial lights or windows. The light is actually shining through the clear crystal walls.

The tunnel empties into a tee at the base of another wall. The cross street gently slopes upward to both left and right. The wall we're facing, which towers high above our heads, appears to be the foundation for the next level up in the city. As we get closer to it, I am reminded of the underground foundation stones of the Temple Mount I saw in Jerusalem, except that this wall looks like it is made of giant slabs of sapphire. It's remarkable!

Standing near the wall at the intersection is a woman dressed from head to foot in bright scarlet. The color seems twice as vibrant against the blue wall behind her.

As we get closer, we see that the fabric of her robe includes a pattern with shades of red, purple, and black. Around her waist is wrapped a long scarlet cord with fringed ends.

When we look at her face, we're surprised to see makeup. Her eyelids are a light purple, her lips a vivid red. She wears large gold hoop earrings and a gold necklace hangs around her neck. Several gold rings adorn her fingers. A shock of blonde hair peeks from under her head covering.

"I see by your reaction that I'm not what you expected. You're surprised by my appearance," says the woman in red. "Well, let me tell you something: *God's story is full of surprises.*"

A Series of Surprises

"My name is Rahab. Yes, that Rahab, once a prostitute but later the mother of Boaz and the great-great-grandmother of King David. You may be surprised to meet me, but I can tell you that no one was more surprised than I was by the events that occurred in Jericho at the hands of the Living God.

"I was an outcast in my family, left destitute, with no way to provide for myself. So I did what I had to do to survive. I sold myself to men who passed through the city. Jericho was a great city in those days. We traded with people from far and near, so everyone was prosperous. But then the rumors began to circulate, and many of the regular merchants stopped coming to the city. The story was that a people who belonged to a Living God were coming from across the Jordan River, and they intended to conquer everyone in their path.

"The walls of Jericho were legendary." She looks at her surroundings. "Of course, they were nothing compared to these. But they were strong for their time. I and everyone else in the city believed no army could conquer those walls. However, when the rumors started, I began to hear amazing things that arrested my attention."

"I Was Surprised When I Heard the Story of God Parting the Red Sea"

"It was said that this people had fled the mighty kingdom of Egypt when God parted the sea, allowing them to walk across dry land to safety, and God had drowned Pharaoh's mighty army when they tried to follow."

"I Was Surprised When I Heard the Powerful Amorite Kings Had Been Destroyed"

"The people of Jericho were acquainted with the powerful kings Sihon and Og because we traded with their people. They both had powerful armies, and did whatever they pleased. Yet we heard that the Children of Israel had fought against them and wiped them out. We couldn't believe it. Fear ran through the city of Jericho. And I knew deep down in my soul that these followers of God would someday be coming with the intention of defeating us."

"I Was Surprised When the Spies Appeared on My Doorstep"

"When two strangers came to Jericho and approached me, I thought they were like all the other men who sought me out. I was shocked when I realized they were Israelites who had been sent by their leader to assess Jericho's defenses. But I could tell that God was with them, and when they asked for my help, I gave it to them. I hid them from the king's men in my house built into the walls of the city. And I helped them escape. I threw the king off their scent by sending his men in the wrong direction. In turn, the Israelite spies swore to protect me and my family—but only if I tied a scarlet cord in the window." She looks down and fingers the belt around her waist. "This very cord. I wear it in remembrance."

"I Was Surprised When the Israelites Kept Their Promise to Spare Me and My Family"

"The day that the Israelites showed up outside of the city, I knew it was only a matter of time before they found a way in. That very day I went to my parents, my brothers, and my sisters and told them to stay with me in my house. They refused. They wanted nothing to do with me, and they boasted about Jericho's impenetrable walls. The next day the result was the same. But by the third day they began to look worried. One of my brothers came to stay with me. Then another. Then a sister. On the sixth day, my father declared that all of us would wait there together. And on the seventh day, God brought down the walls.

"As we huddled together in my room listening to the sounds of people being slaughtered outside my door, I wondered if this God and His followers could really be trusted. When there was loud pounding on the door, we feared the worst. But God was faithful. The spies who had made the promise escorted us out of the city before they burned it to the ground."

"I Was Surprised to Be Included in the Bloodline of Jesus"

The greatest surprise of all was that I—the one people called Rahab the whore—was considered righteous by God,[8] married Salmon, and became the great-grandmother, twenty-eight generations removed, of Jesus, the Messiah and Savior of mankind."[9]

God Is the Master of Surprises

Many people express surprise that God would include a harlot in the bloodline of Jesus, but if you think about it, you can see that the Bible is really one long record of God-surprises. Noah was surprised when God ordered him to build an ark and saved him and his family from the flood that destroyed the world. Abraham and Sarah were surprised when God gave them a son in their old age. Moses was surprised by the burning bush. The Children of Israel were surprised when God rolled back the waters of the Jordan to allow them to march into the Promised Land. The people of the Holy Land were surprised when Elijah called fire down on Mount Carmel. And the entire world was surprised when God sent Jesus, His only Son, down to earth to redeem mankind.

We've all heard the old cliché "God moves in mysterious ways." It's probably more accurate to say that God specializes in surprising us. A God-surprise...

- is unexpected and unexplainable,
- disrupts the status quo,
- turns the ordinary into the spectacular,
- shows you how much bigger God is than what you have known or seen,
- changes your expectations and your destiny, and
- leaves no room for doubt—God is God.

The only thing in life that should not surprise us is that God will surprise us. He delights in doing so. If God's mind were small enough for us to understand, He wouldn't be God.

Life Lessons from Rahab

As we think about God's surprises, Rahab begins to speak again and shares the wisdom of her experience:

"God Invites You to Be Part of His Story—Join Him"

"Every person's life is a story with the potential for drama and humor, tragedy and triumph. My life was an amazing story. Your life is also a story. How will it turn out? Anyone who turns to God is invited to be part of His story, and that is the most amazing thing of all. God is extending to you an invitation to be part of something bigger.

"I was a member of a race God told the Children of Israel to wipe out, yet He still invited me to be part of His story. In fact, I was part of His *greatest* story, the sending of Jesus to save the world. You can be part of that same story if you choose to join God and follow His leading."

"God Wants to Surprise You with His Love—Accept Him"

"I did not expect God to love me. I was an outcast. Even my own family rejected me. But God did love me. That was a surprise. I only had to choose to accept His love.

"Do you know how much God loves you? He loves each of us as if there were only one of us. His love is real, and His offer to be your God is always on the table. Do you doubt it? If so, then every day tell yourself that God loves you as you are—not as you wish you were. Not as others think you are. As you are right now. And you cannot change that. You cannot make Him love you more. You cannot make Him love you less. His love is His love. I hope you accept it, as I did."

"God Asks You to Surprise Others with Your Actions—Obey Him"

"My acceptance of the spies surprised my family. They thought I was foolish to aid an enemy and to defy the king. Their reaction was motivated by fear. Mine was motivated by love. I took action because I believed in the Living God they served, the God I now serve—my God and Savior. I acted to save the spies, but God used that action to save me. And that's often how God works. We serve others unselfishly out of obedience to Him, and God uses our own actions to help us. It is our business to do what's right; it's God's business to make sure everything turns out right. Obeying God placed me in His care, and what He gave me—a place in Jesus's lineage—was mine forever.

"What is God currently asking you to do for someone else? Don't question Him. Don't doubt Him. Just obey Him. You have no idea what God might be up to. It's not what you do that matters as much as what God does through you. God doesn't want your busyness. He wants your obedience. The Kingdom of God is a paradox. Through a prostitute God received glory. What might He do through you?"

"When God Performs a Miracle, He Is Signing His Name to Your Story—Celebrate Him"

"My life story did not start out well. The life of sin I chose promised so much but produced so little. It is a miracle that God spared my life. I was a Canaanite and a prostitute. I and my family alone were the only survivors of Jericho. But it's an even greater miracle that God allowed me to be Jesus's grandmother twenty-eight generations removed. God looked at my broken life and saw a masterpiece. I learned that anything less than God will let you down.

"Sometimes we get to *see* the miracle. Others times we get to *be* the miracle. When God surprised me by performing a miracle, it was like He was signing His name to my story. Others dismissed me, but God believed I was miracle material. And as a result, my name has been remembered for millennia.

"Think about the things God has done for you. It is His way of signing His name to your story. Celebrate Him for that by giving Him your all. Praise His holy name."

The Prayer of Rahab

Rahab closes her eyes for a moment, and then she begins to pray:

"O Living God Who Loves Us,

"When you look at these friends, You see a masterpiece in the making, just as You saw one in me. I celebrate that their lives are yet unfinished stories because it means there is still room for Your surprises. I pray that every day they will allow themselves to be part of Your greater story and that they will allow the surprises You provide to ring through eternity. Amen."

Rahab looks at us one more time and says, "The next person you will meet will be here shortly. Wait for her here. And remember: make your story great!"

Leadership Lessons from Rahab

Rahab's enthusiasm is contagious. She makes me want to be better than I am, to make my life count for God. And her visit gets me thinking about leadership, and the lessons we can learn from her.

1. Good Leaders Recognize When God Is Moving

When the people of Canaan heard the stories about the Israelites, they grew fearful. Not Rahab. She recognized that God was moving. He was doing something, and she prepared herself to become a part of it.

Good leaders learn how to read every situation and understand what's going on. And when those leaders are people of faith, they must become sensitive to the Holy Spirit and be aware of how God is moving. They read and respond in appropriate ways.

When I was the senior pastor of Skyline Church, I reminded myself of this every Sunday before the service by reciting this prayer: "God, this is Your church, not mine. You are in control, not me. My agenda is human; Yours is divine. I submit myself to Your agenda. When You move, I promise to move with You. My movements without You are nothing but wood, hay, and stubble. Your movements are life-changing."

If you lead people, make yourself aware of what God is doing. Submit to Him. Be sensitive to Him. Let go of your agenda, and when He moves, move along with Him.

2. Good Leaders Don't Allow the Fear of Others to Overcome Their Judgment

There were several times Rahab could have let fear overwhelm her—when the word came to Jericho about how God was helping the Israelites conquer other kings, when the spies showed up at her door, when the king sent leaders to seek out the spies. But she didn't. She kept her wits about her, helped the spies to escape from the locked-down city, and even advised them on how to evade capture and get back to their people safely. She showed good leadership skills under pressure.

Whenever we face risk or uncertainty, fear can be a problem. But as someone once pointed out, fear is a fruit, not the root of the problem. Inaction comes from lack of belief, not from fear itself. God is faithful. When He says He will do something, He always follows through.

We should learn from Rahab's example. We can't allow fear or pressure to cloud our judgment. We must fight fear with faith. We must overcome inaction with belief. It's no mistake that the Bible contains the admonition to "fear not" 365 times—one for every day of the year. Remember, people are always depending on leaders because they have the capacity to see before others do, to see farther than others do, and to see more clearly than others do. If leaders lose that capacity, then they should no longer lead, because everyone will suffer.

3. Good Leaders Always Use the Advantages God Gives Them to Help Others

When Rahab received favor from God and the spies, she used it to save her entire family—her mother, father, brothers, and sisters, and all who belonged to them. She recognized that the advantages she received from leading well were not just for herself.

If you lead others, you need to ask yourself why you do it. Is it for personal recognition? Is it to receive the benefits? Does it make you feel better about yourself? Or are you doing it to benefit others, to make their stories better and to bring glory to God? Why you lead is as important as what you do as a leader.

As we wait for the next giant of the faith, we think about Rahab's message—that God's story is full of surprises—and I reflect on how true that has been in my life. I still cannot believe how God has blessed me with a great family, wonderful friends, influence upon others, and success beyond the wildest dreams of my youth. I don't deserve any of it, but I am certainly grateful for it. And it's inspiring to be reminded that my story isn't finished yet. I can't wait to find out what God has for me next.

Woman to Woman

In thinking about Rahab, I am reminded that God's plan is an intricate puzzle that none of us could ever understand. Who wouldn't feel encouraged, inspired, and intrigued in thinking about this unwanted, unloved woman who is part of the lineage of our Savior?

Rahab gave the only thing she had, which was her faith. By faith even Rahab was saved. We are fond of saying, "Come just as you are." Rahab came, and she was delivered. I love that even in my unlovable moments, God is sovereign and still has a plan for my life. And even in the unlovable moments of the people around me, God is sovereign and still has a plan for their lives. God is gracious.

I can't wait to sit at the feet of Jesus and hear the many stories of how He has used the most unexpected, unfit people to save thousands and bring the lost into His kingdom!

Rahab reminds me that God welcomes me and has a plan for me.

—Jenn Richards

Questions for Reflection or Discussion

To learn more about Rahab, read Joshua 2:1–24 and 6:20–25, Matthew 1:5, Hebrews 11:31, and James 2:25.

1. Have you ever thought of your life as a story? If you were asked to describe it as one, how would you do so? You may want to compare it to a familiar movie, play, or book.
2. Well-told stories have a beginning, middle, and end. Which part of your story are you currently living? Explain.
3. How would you like your story to end? Describe it.
4. Do you believe that God still does miracles today? Why or why not?
5. What would it mean for you to join God's story in a way you haven't before?
6. Where is God currently moving in your life? If you're not sure, ask others if they can sense it.
7. What action is God currently asking you to take? Describe how you feel about it, and are you willing to take that step?

HANNAH

God Blesses the Promises You Keep to Him

Rahab told us to wait here for the next person, so we wait. It gives us some time to view our surroundings. I look more closely at the wall made of clear stone of a vivid blue. Each slab is larger than a railroad car. The sides are perfectly straight and smooth, the corners perfect. They are fitted together so tightly I don't think I would even be able to slide a piece of paper between them.

I look down and realize that the street we stand on appears to be made of the same hard crystal material the walls are made of. It too looks perfect.

I'm dying to do some exploring. We wait a few more minutes, and then I can stand it no longer. Nearby is a stairway built into the great city wall. We just *have* to climb it and take a look around.

It takes much longer than I expected for us to make our way up to the top of the stairway. I have no idea how high we've climbed, but when we do finally get to the top, I'm out of breath.

The wall is much wider than I expected, but then I remember how long it took us to walk through the tunnel under it. We walk out onto the top of the wall, which is like a parade ground, except that instead of being made of dirt or grass, the surface is of the clear stone that made up the foundation of the wall. Here there are also geometric patterns made of brightly colored stones inlaid in the surface. It's beautiful.

We stop and look back toward the city and realize that it is built in levels, one rising up above the next. Each level has a foundation and wall of its own. The lowest level is widest, and each level above it is slightly smaller. It rises so high I can't see the top.

We walk across the wall toward the outer edge. The view is incredible. We can see the meadow we crossed to get to the city. There are forests and valleys and streams below us. I wonder if the Garden of Eden looked anything like what we're seeing.

As we gaze out beyond the walls, we hear the voice of someone behind us. "I see you couldn't resist coming up to look at the view," she says. "It's quite beautiful, isn't it?"

We turn and see a rather small middle-aged woman dressed in a simple gray cloak. She has a kind face that reminds me of my mother.

"Let's walk along the wall as we talk," she says. She walks to the left so that the meadow is on our left and the city on our right.

Prompted to Pray

"What is your greatest wish?" she asks. "What is the deepest longing of your soul, the thing you believe you were put on earth to do?" Her words hang in the air for a moment. I begin to search for my answer, but before I am able to articulate it, she continues speaking. "I lived the first half of my life with that dream unfulfilled. And I feared that perhaps it would never be fulfilled. What does one do in that situation?"

Again she leaves us with the question, prompting us to think. And again, before we can respond, she speaks. "I am Hannah," she says, "and I want to explain some very important things to you about the promises we make to God."

"Most People Make Bold Promises to God During Times of Pressure and Desperation"

"I know this because I was one of them. You see, every day, year after year, Elkanah's other wife, Peninnah, humiliated me because she had children and I did not. It crushed me and made me sick to my stomach. I often felt so terrible I could not even eat. In desperation I promised God that if He would give me a son, I would dedicate the boy to Him. Not only that, but I would dedicate him as a Nazirite, one set apart from all others.

"Sometimes when we're desperate and we make promises to God, we believe that we need to sweeten the deal to get God to give us what we want. That's what I did. I hoped God would not be able to resist such a deal. But God cannot be bribed. He has no need for anything we could possibly offer. When God says yes to our request, it is for our benefit, not His."

"Many People Feel a Sense of Relief After Prayer"

"After I prayed in the Temple court, asking God for a son, and after Eli prayed for me and blessed me, I felt better. I no longer felt the deep grief I had before, and I could finally eat again.

"Many people use prayer as a means of release. They pray and feel relief. The greater the pressure, the more desperate the prayer—and the greater the relief when they unburden themselves. But prayer is more than just a release—a mental or spiritual way to relieve pressure. It is interaction with the Living God of the universe, the Author of all things. We must never forget that or take it for granted!"

"Some People Remember Their Promise After the Pressure Has Been Lifted"

"How many desperate prayers have we prayed in our lives? How many promises have we made to God when we were afraid, guilty, sick, or crushed in spirit? Even the most hardened skeptic prays when he is desperate enough. Yet how many people forget those prayers once they are no longer afraid or distraught? How many forget the God Who helped them after the time of danger or distress?

"When I realized I was pregnant, my heart leaped for joy. My lifelong dream was finally being fulfilled. I could finally face Peninnah and hold my head up high. I could finally see joy added to love in the eyes of Elkanah, instead of sympathy. I would be a mother at last!

"Knowing that, how could I forget the One Who made

it possible? I did not forget my promise to God. And if you have made a promise to God, neither should you."

"Few People Follow Through and Keep Their Promises to God"

"When we pray for something and make a big promise to God—and He delivers—we have a significant decision to make. Will we keep our promise?

"When I gave birth to Samuel, I did not know if God would ever grant me another child. Truthfully, I worried that He wouldn't. And I started thinking, *What will happen to me? If I give up Samuel, who will care for me in my old age, after Elkanah is gone? Surely Peninnah's children will not lift a finger to help me.*

"I knew there was a very good chance I would become a destitute widow. *Does God ask us to keep a promise that may put us in such difficult circumstances?* I wondered. *Doesn't He make exceptions?* To that I have only one thing to say: *God blesses the promises you keep to Him.*"

Life Lessons from Hannah

Hannah lets her words soak in as we walk with her at a leisurely pace. Her slow steady speech seems to match our gait. She is in no hurry. She speaks with an easy confidence, like a veteran teacher whose tone says that she has our best interests at heart and wants to make sure we don't miss an important lesson.

I start thinking about the times in my life when I've made promises to God under pressure, but before I have time to reflect, Hannah is speaking again:

"When You Keep Your Promise to God, He Blesses You with Joy"

"When I became pregnant, I was ecstatic. I cannot describe what it meant to have a child growing inside me when I had been desperate for one for so long. For nine months I wondered, would it be a girl that I could keep? Or would it be a boy that I would need to dedicate to God? I admit I had mixed feelings. Every woman of my time wanted a son to carry on the family name and to stand in his father's place when he went to be with the Lord. But I knew that if God gave me a girl, I would be able to keep her.

"When my Samuel was born, I was overjoyed. But I also knew what it meant. My boy was only on loan to me. He belonged to God. I knew I would follow through. I would dedicate him to God, and not merely the way the Law instructed, by offering a sacrifice in his place. I would *truly* give him to God. After Samuel was weaned, I delivered him to Eli in Shiloh so that he could serve God in His house all the days of his life. And God accepted him, even though he was not a Levite, not from the tribe of priests.

"I told you I felt relief and joy the day Eli prayed for me at the Temple. And I felt joy the day I realized I was pregnant. Believe it or not, I felt just as much joy the day I departed from the house of God and left my son behind in the care of Eli. Few things in this life return as much joy as cheerful obedience to God."

"When You Keep Your Promise Wholeheartedly, God Blesses You by Giving Back to You"

"When I gave Samuel to God, I didn't know what my future held. But God was kind to me. He blessed me with three more sons and two daughters. I lived a fulfilling life as a mother, grandmother, and great-grandmother.

"God always gives back to us when we give to Him. He does not promise to give back in kind. He never told me He would give me another son to replace the one I gave Him. But God always gives back in some way. You cannot out-give God."

"When You Keep Your Promise for Your Reasons, God Blesses Others for His Reasons"

"My prayer to God was very personal. I wanted to experience giving birth and nursing a baby. I wanted to know the fulfillment of being a mother. And my promise to Him was also personal. But God took what was personal to me and used it as a gift to bless others:

"God blessed my beloved husband Elkanah with more sons and daughters.

"God blessed Eli with a good 'son' and spiritual heir to replace his two wicked sons.

"God blessed Samuel by allowing him to become a true priest and a prophet who served God faithfully for all his life.

"God blessed all of Israel because her children enjoyed one of the nation's best leaders.

"I never doubted the sovereignty of God, but I also had no idea how much God could do with my single act of obedience.

"Never underestimate God. You have no idea how many blessings He will shower on others when you keep your promises to Him. Your grateful obedience not only shows God your love; it also frees Him to use you to bless others and do His will."

The Prayer of Hannah

Hannah stops walking and faces us. With each of her hands she grabs one of ours. "Eli prayed for me that day so many years ago," she says, "and now, like him, I shall pray for you." With a strong, confident voice she says,

> *"O God Our Provider,*
>> *"Do not allow my friends to forget the promises they have made to You. When You give them the desires of their hearts, bring their promises to mind, and give them the heart and the will to fulfill those promises. And may others be bountifully blessed by their cheerful and grateful obedience to You. Amen."*

Hannah exudes a quiet confidence as she smiles at us. "You will go to the second level of the city to meet the next person. Instead of going back down the way you came, keep walking in this direction along the top of this wall, and you will soon come to a bridge on your right. Walk across it back toward the heart of the city. She will be waiting for you at the end of the bridge." With that she releases our hands and sends us on our way.

Leadership Lessons from Hannah

As we walk in the direction Hannah indicated, we reflect on her words and the wisdom contained in them. And I recognize that leadership insight can be gained from her:

1. When You Are Faithful to God, He Fights for You

When Hannah left Samuel at the house of God, she didn't mourn. She celebrated. Her prayer starts with the words,

> I'm bursting with GOD-news!
> I'm walking on air.
> I'm laughing at my rivals.
> I'm dancing my salvation.[10]

Why was she so happy? Certainly her faithfulness to God had brought her great fulfillment. But there was also another reason. She recognized that God had fought for her, which He always does for those who are faithful to Him. In her prayer she speaks of God smashing the weapons of the strong and infusing the weak with strength, feeding the hungry, and giving children to the barren. She sums up her perspective by saying,

> GOD's enemies will be blasted out of the sky,
> crashed in a heap and burned.
> GOD will set things right all over the earth.[11]

God fought for Hannah, and He wants to fight for you. As you lead others, remain faithful to God because it makes you a candidate for God's favor.

2. When You Are Faithful to God, He Also Blesses the People You Lead

After the Hebrews arrived in the Promised Land and Joshua died, the leadership of Israel was at best inconsistent. Judges records how occasionally a good leader such as Deborah or Gideon would emerge, but most of the time the leaders were weak or nonexistent. As a result the people of Israel were unfaithful to God, and their enemies dominated them. The last words recorded in the book of Judges describe the situation leading up to Hannah's era: "At that time there was no king in Israel. People did whatever they felt like doing."[12]

Even the leadership of God's tabernacle was in shambles. Eli was a faithful priest, but he did not provide good leadership. His two corrupt sons violated God's precepts for the Levites, yet Eli did nothing.

Into this leadership-starved atmosphere arrived Samuel, through the faithful obedience of Hannah's kept promise. Samuel too was faithful to God, and it wasn't long before his influence grew and blessed the people of Israel. Scripture says,

> Samuel grew up. GOD was with him, and Samuel's prophetic record was flawless. Everyone in Israel, from Dan in the north to Beersheba in the south, recognized that Samuel was the real thing—a true prophet of GOD. GOD continued to show up at Shiloh, revealed through his word to Samuel at Shiloh.[13]

Samuel became the voice of God for the people. He directed and advised them. During his lifetime he established kings and helped Israel achieve victory over its enemies. Samuel served many roles in his lifetime and all of them were influential. Hannah's obedience affected many generations in Israel.

3. When You Are Faithful to God, He Multiplies Your Impact

What might have happened if Hannah had decided to keep Samuel for herself? Or if Elkanah had not said, "Let God complete what he has begun!"[14] when Hannah stated her intention to dedicate Samuel to God after he was weaned? No one but God knows. But we do know this: because Hannah faithfully fulfilled her promise to God, the entire nation of Israel benefited. The Israelites resisted the Philistines, who wanted to enslave them. The people were challenged to turn from idolatry by Samuel. And David was anointed king over Israel and unified the tribes into a single mighty nation.

When we look at Hannah's sacrifice of her own son for God's greater purpose, we realize that the people of the Old Testament received a glimpse of what God intended to do when He gave His own Son for us.

If you're a mother or father, you need to understand that your child could be the next Samuel. You have no idea what God may do with your children. So raise them well. Train them up in the way they should go. And release them to fulfill their God-given purpose when the time comes.

Woman to Woman

I love the name of Hannah and the story that goes along with it. Turns out my parents did too, since they named me after the Hannah in the Bible. I am only thirteen and I don't have much experience with making promises to God. But last year, when my dad was really sick, I prayed out of desperation. I really needed an answer to my prayer and I wasn't going to stop praying for it. I guess my persistence makes me a little like her.

Hannah prayed and made a promise to God out of desperation. For years she didn't have any children and was reminded of that by Elkanah's other wife. She also made a promise to get God's attention. I think Hannah probably thought her promise would sweeten the deal a little too.

The first lesson I am learning from Hannah is to always put God first in my life, even when it's hard. The second lesson I'm learning is that only God can meet my deepest needs. Whenever I need to make a promise to God, I will remember Hannah, and try to live up to my name.

—Hannah Maxwell

Questions for Reflection or Discussion

To learn more about Hannah, read 1 Samuel 1:1–2:21.

1. Hannah was made to feel bad by Peninnah. Have you ever been in a position where someone belittled you because they said you lacked some quality, possession, or advantage that they had? How did it make you feel? How did you respond?

2. When you feel discouraged and someone attempts to encourage you, as Elkanah tried to do with Hannah, does it help you? How do you ordinarily respond? Why do you react as you do?

3. Do you currently have a deep desire for something, similar to Hannah's desire for a child? If so, what is it?

4. What would it mean to you if God fulfilled that desire?

5. Have you ever made a promise to God when you were in trouble or distress? If so, what was it? Did you keep it, or choose not to follow through, or forget about it when it was time to fulfill it? Explain.

6. Is there a promise that God is currently reminding you about? If so, are you willing to follow through with it?

7. How can others assist you as you strive to be faithful to God?

ABIGAIL

*A Single Act of Wisdom Can Change
Your Destiny*

We walk along the wall, and it isn't long before we see the bridge ahead on our right. It's extraordinary. The bridge is built in a long, graceful arch that spans the space between the top of the wall and the second level of the city. We can see that the bridge is not made of the same material as the wall, but from a distance, it's difficult to recognize what its color actually is. As we get closer, we can see that the structure isn't just a single color. It's layers of different colors in bands—purple, pink, orange, yellow, and white. The colors and pattern remind me of a beautiful geode I saw in a museum, with its multilayered patterns of crystal. Some of the bands are wide, others narrow, and they appear to be perfectly straight and level.

When we finally arrive at the bridge, we get a sense of how big it is. Four or five cars would be able to drive over it side by side. It rises gently toward its center. As we walk on the bridge, the curve of the surface exposes the bands of colored stone. They are spectacular. And then it occurs to me that there are no joints or seams anywhere to be seen in the entire bridge. The structure is made of a single massive piece of stone!

I'm so distracted that I nearly run into a couple who are walking along in the opposite direction. The woman is dressed in an odd outfit made of a weird shimmering kind of fabric. Her shoes are transparent. The man is dressed only in a loincloth and walks on bare feet.

I apologize, and refocus my attention forward. That's when I start to make out the buildings beyond the bridge. They glimmer. I realize they are made of gold.

Even before we get close to the end of the bridge, we can see her. She stands out like a jewel set in gold, like a beautiful amethyst. She wears a long cloak made of a vibrant violet fabric. Her posture is erect. The word that immediately comes to mind is *dignified*. When we get close enough, we can see that she wears a golden necklace. Rings adorn her fingers. And in her hair are combs adorned with jewels. But these are nothing compared to her beauty. Surely this woman must be a queen.

"Greetings to you, my friends," she says. Her voice is beautiful, like a song. "I am delighted to meet you. I have been looking forward to our time together. Shall we walk?" She asks it as a polite question, but her confidence and tone leave no room for any answer but yes.

"My father thought he was doing me a favor when he arranged my marriage to a wealthy and well-established man whose household was huge. But my husband was a cruel man, stingy and full of his own self-importance. I and everyone else in his life suffered because of his shortsightedness and his petty leadership.

"For years I did everything in my power to try to help him and to win him over, but nothing worked. I resigned myself to enduring him and making the most of a bad situation. But then Nabal did something that was foolish even by his standards. He insulted David, God's anointed, and treated his men with contempt. He doomed us. He put our entire household in a no-win situation. But let me tell you something," she says, pausing for emphasis. *"A single act of wisdom can change your destiny."*

When Wisdom and Action Come Together

The wife of Nabal. This is none other than Abigail. No wonder she speaks with such command and intelligence. Her wisdom in an extremely difficult situation was exceptional. David sent ten young men to ask Nabal for food during the sheep-shearing celebration, since David's men had protected Nabal's shepherds. But Nabal responded by saying,

> Who is this David? Who is this son of Jesse? The country is full of runaway servants these days. Do you think I'm going to take good bread and wine and meat freshly butchered for my sheep-shearers and give it to men I've never laid eyes on? Who knows where they've come from?[15]

Nabal's insults infuriated David, who responded by commanding four hundred of his battle-hardened men to arm themselves and travel to Maon near Carmel, where Nabal lived. But Abigail's wisdom and grace in the face of danger were exceptional.

Abigail Had the Wisdom to Listen to the Young Shepherd

The word of what had happened between Nabal and David's men came to Abigail through a young shepherd who had benefited from the protection of David. He understood how powerful David and his men were, and he warned Abigail of impending disaster.

To her credit, Abigail didn't discount or dismiss what the shepherd said because he was young or because his status was lowly. She took in everything he said and quickly assessed the situation the entire household was facing.

Abigail Had the Wisdom to Take Immediate Action

Many people when confronted with genuine danger are paralyzed by fear. They can become racked with indecision or outright freeze up. Not Abigail. Scripture says,

> Abigail flew into action. She took two hundred loaves of bread, two skins of wine, five sheep dressed out and ready for cooking, a bushel of roasted grain, a hundred raisin cakes, and two hundred fig cakes, and she had it all loaded on some donkeys. Then she said to her young servants, "Go ahead and pave the way for me. I'm right behind you." But she said nothing to her husband, Nabal.[16]

Abigail knew that David needed food and supplies. That's what he'd had his men ask for. So she quickly selected provisions, probably from what her husband was preparing to feast upon himself, and sent them on ahead of her in a way reminiscent of how Jacob sent gifts to his brother Esau before crossing the Jordan River to face him.

Abigail Had the Wisdom to Act with Humility

Abigail bore no blame for the foolish actions of her husband, yet she humbled herself before David, falling to her knees and putting her face to the ground. "My master, let me take the blame!" she said. "Don't dwell on what that brute Nabal did. He acts out the meaning of his name: Nabal, Fool. Foolishness oozes from him."[17] Abigail grabbed David's attention with her humility and submission. Perhaps some of the words David wrote in the Psalms,

> The Lord preserves those who are true to him,
> but the proud he pays back in full,[18]

were inspired by the humble words and actions of Abigail and what occurred afterward.

Abigail Had the Wisdom to Put Things into Perspective for David

Once Abigail had David's attention and had started to defuse his anger by providing food for him and his men, she spoke with great wisdom and clarity, helping David to see things from God's perspective, saying,

> My master fights GOD's battles! As long as you live no evil will stick to you.... Your GOD-honored life is tightly bound in the bundle of GOD-protected life; But the lives of your enemies will be hurled aside as a stone is thrown from a sling.
>
> When GOD completes all the goodness he has promised my master and sets you up as prince over Israel, my master will not have this dead weight in his heart, the guilt of an avenging murder.[19]

David was instantly reminded of his true mission and recognized the truth of what Abigail said.

Abigail Had the Wisdom to Ask for David's Favor

Abigail's main goals were to save the people of her household from destruction and to guide David away from revenge so that he would not become distracted from his God-given mission of fighting God's battles. However, she didn't stop there. She asked for David's favor, saying, "And when GOD has worked things for good for my master, remember me."[20]

Perhaps Abigail knew that the foolishness and mean-ness of her husband would inevitably lead to trouble, so she was planning ahead for such a time. At any rate, David recognized her intelligence and value, acknowledging that God Himself had sent Abigail to change his heart.

It's small wonder that when David learned a few days later that Nabal had died, he again acknowledged, "Blessed be GOD who has stood up for me against Nabal's insults, kept me from an evil act, and let Nabal's evil boomerang back on him."[21] David immediately sent for Abigail, asking that she become his wife.

Life Lessons from Abigail

The more I think about Abigail's story, the more I am in awe of her. I can't contain myself, and I feel that I have to tell her.

"You displayed such fantastic leadership," I say. "With a single action, you did so many things. You saved your household. You prevented a blood feud that would have erupted between David and his followers, and the family of Nabal within the tribe of Caleb. And you prevented God's anointed leader from becoming distracted from his calling."

Abigail eyes me and responds, "True. I also changed my destiny and that of my future children. I was well cared for, my children were the offspring of a godly man, and I had the honor of serving as a queen of Israel. And there are some things you can learn from this."

"Wisdom Paired with Action Gets Positive Results"

"What use is wisdom without action? It is like a jewel left buried in the ground, a gift thoughtfully given but left unopened, a meal beautifully prepared and laid, but left uneaten. It's a terrible waste. As a result of that pairing, nothing is accomplished, nothing changes.

"What use is action without wisdom? It's like a storm that rages on the sea, having power but accomplishing nothing positive or constructive. At best it leads to a hollow busyness. At worst it creates destruction.

"However, when wisdom is paired with action, it can save families, beat back hostile armies, bring together enemies. It can change the world. One of the things that made my husband David great was how often he paired action with wisdom and allowed them to be guided by love."

"When Taking Action, Do the Right Thing the Right Way"

"When I threw myself at the feet of my lord, David, I was doing the right thing. The actions of Nabal had been foolish and mean, but had not violated God's Law in a way that warranted a death sentence. By intervening on his behalf, I not only saved Nabal and the people of our household, I also kept David from a grievous error.

"I suppose I could have acted with indignation. I could have lectured David and cited the Law. But even the right thing done the wrong way can lead to disaster. No, just because I was in the right did not mean I was free to act in the wrong. As God's anointed, David deserved my respect, and I was glad to give it to him."

"God Promises to Give You Wisdom if You Ask—So Ask"

"The wisdom I possessed in life was granted to me by God. It was a gift I neither earned nor deserved, yet it served me well. And what's fantastic is that God will generously give it to you, just as He did to David's son Solomon when he asked for it. Many centuries after my time on earth, James, the earthly brother of our Lord Jesus, revealed this promise of God to the Church, telling them, "'If any of you lacks wisdom, you should ask God, who gives generously to all without finding fault, and it will be given to you.'"[22]

Abigail stops and looks as us intently. "Only the foolish, like my first husband, Nabal, do not ask God for wisdom," she says. "So if you have not already asked for wisdom from Him, what are you waiting for?"

The Prayer of Abigail

When Abigail asks this question, we feel prompted to answer. Before either of us has a chance to respond, she begins walking again, and says, "Before I leave you, I feel compelled to pray for you," and she immediately launches in:

> *"All-knowing and All-powerful God,*
>
> *"We gladly acknowledge that a reverent fear of You is the beginning of all wisdom, and we embrace that truth wholeheartedly. I ask that you give these children of Your wisdom—to follow You, to lead others, and to fulfill their purpose. We are grateful that through our requests and our acts of obedience You allow us to change history and the destiny of ourselves and others. May they always act with Your wisdom. Amen."*

Leadership Lessons from Abigail

"To meet your next mentor, you need only walk up this street," says Abigail, pointing in the direction we have been walking. "When you've reached the right place, you'll know it."

She is so charismatic and her words so engaging that I've hardly paid attention to our surroundings as we've walked. As I look where she is pointing, I see the buildings that line the road on either side. Their bright, reflective surfaces look like polished gold, and their beauty makes me speechless. Before I'm able to thank Abigail, or indeed to say anything at all, she has left us.

As you and I walk along the street, passing one golden structure after another, we think about the leadership wisdom we can glean from Abigail.

1. Leaders Need to Possess the Right Perspective

Even though David was a powerful leader and was anointed to become king, it was Abigail who brought the right perspective to him. She saw the bigger picture. She thought through the consequences of David's intended actions. She had a sense of what God desired from both of them in that situation. And she looked to the future, not only for herself but for others.

If you are a leader, you must always seek God's wisdom, take the long view, and attempt to see the big picture. In addition, you cannot allow your emotions to overwhelm your judgment. You must maintain your perspective. The people you lead are depending on you.

2. Leaders Must Take Initiative

While it was true that Nabal was the head of the household, he was not the true leader. Abigail was. She understood the predicament all of them were in, and she rightly judged that if she did not take action, the result would be catastrophic for everyone.

I strongly believe that good leaders see things before others do. That ability is largely God-given. Why does God grant that ability? So that leaders can act. I have yet to observe an effective leader who did not take initiative. If you lead other people, it is your responsibility to look for problems and solutions, to connect with people and get to know them, to gather a team and move it forward. These things do not happen on their own.

3. Leaders Know to Appeal to the Whole Person

Abigail was wise enough to appeal to David's heart, mind, and even stomach. She knew he was angry and hungry. She gave him food, knowing she was addressing his physical needs and those of his warriors. But she also knew she needed to help him feel the right emotions. Instead of anger, she wanted him to feel compassion. By humbling herself, she helped him calm down and connected with him. That made it possible for her to appeal to his common sense, his values, and his heart for God. She also painted a picture of a better future for him. It's a master class in communication. How could David resist?

When you communicate with the people you desire to lead, you need to treat them in a similar way. Pay attention to their physical needs. Can they see and hear you? Are they hungry or uncomfortable? Do they need a break? (No communicator can successfully compete against urgent physical needs.) If there are no physical obstacles, then work to connect with them. Appeal to their hearts first, then their minds, values, and interests. Show them a way to a better future for themselves, and not only will they be open to what you have to say; they may be inspired.

4. Leaders Must Be Bold

Abigail was humble when she confronted David, but she wasn't timid. She addressed him boldly, challenged his thinking, and offered him a different and better path. That took guts. David was a mighty warrior and God's anointed leader. Abigail had no status at all. Yet she spoke clearly and boldly. And that made the difference. How many lives did she save in the process? David had vowed, "May God do his worst to me if Nabal and every cur in his misbegotten brood aren't dead meat by morning!"[23]

Sometimes the only thing standing between people and tragedy is the boldness of a leader. If you have the responsibility of leadership, then be willing to step up and take bold action, not for personal gain or glory, but for the sake of the people you lead.

You may be like Abigail. You may be an exceptional leader who has gone unrecognized. Or you may be someone who possesses no status or official authority. Do not let that stop you from doing the right thing. Never underestimate the power of one small act. Exercise the wisdom God has given you by putting it into action. There's no telling what God may do with it.

Woman to Woman

Whenever I read the story of Abigail, I'm always amazed by how she responded to the foolishness of her husband. She repeatedly found herself dealing with his selfishness, with no way to change his heart. It was a delicate balance to honor him as her husband, without disobeying the Lord. If anyone

(Continued)

could have felt like taking revenge, Abigail could. And she could have easily conspired with David to kill her husband, but that would not have been right.

Instead of wallowing in the misery created by Nabal, she took action. Abigail labored in the kitchen and prepared delicious food, which she immediately sent ahead of her to David. She knew that David and his men were starving and that this was fueling his rage against her husband. The solution she found involved her working with her hands in the kitchen, using the bountiful resources God had already blessed her husband with. Abigail knew God could use this food to help David see beyond his anger and regain some eternal perspective.

The lesson I learn from Abigail as a woman is that wisdom is only as powerful as the gentle action that follows it. Even when the world pulls me in directions that go against God's plan, I can work to be a peacemaker. I should never hesitate to deliver a message of truth when I can package it with love and grace. Instead each of us can serve up a generous portion of wisdom that will leave everyone wanting seconds.

—Elisabeth Maxwell

Questions for Reflection or Discussion

To learn more about Abigail, read 1 Samuel 25:2–42, 27:3, and 30:5, 2 Samuel 2:2 and 3:3, and 1 Chronicles 3:1.

1. Why do you think Abigail was able to so quickly process the news the young shepherd gave her and make the difficult decision of what to do?
2. How quickly are you able to process information and make decisions under pressure?
3. When you find yourself in what feels like a no-win situation, as Abigail did in her marriage to a foolish and bad man, how do you naturally tend to respond?
4. Have you ever been in a situation where you could see certain disaster coming? What did you do? What was the outcome?
5. Can you point to a pivotal decision and action in your life that changed your direction or destiny? What brought you to that decision?
6. How did your life change afterward?
7. Is there a decision you believe God is currently asking you to make? What wisdom are you seeking from God and mature fellow believers?

MIRIAM

Don't Let Comparison Rob You of Your Joy

We walk along the street in the direction Abigail indicated. It seems to run perfectly straight, and it stretches out as far as the eye can see. I wonder how long it is. And what did Abigail mean when she said we would know the place when we saw it?

I remember hearing about the streets of gold in heaven when I was a child. My father, Melvin, preached about them once. But as it turns out, this street is made of stone—the same material the bridge was made of. Only the buildings are gold. As we walk along, we have time to look at them. There seem to be structures of every shape, size, and style. Georgian mansions next to pagodas next to modern geometric marvels next to brownstones next to cabins next to haciendas next to structures that look like they were inspired by tents.

I slow down so that I can take them in as we pass by,

and I can't help thinking that I wish Margaret were with me so she could enjoy them too.

After we've walked for maybe fifteen or twenty minutes, we notice that there is some kind of a gap in the houses up ahead on the left. As we get closer, we see that the opening is wide. When we get there we discover that it is one side of a large square laid out like a park. The other three sides are lined with mansions that overlook the park.

The area is filled with lush and colorful flower beds laid out in geometric shapes. Low miniature hedges, maybe a foot and a half tall, divide the areas. Stone-paved paths crisscross the park among the flower beds.

In the center of the park is a circle of date palm trees. Within the circle is a round raised pool perhaps a hundred feet across with a low stone wall encircling it. In the center of the pool stands a large fountain with water cascading down it. Scattered here and there in the pool are plants with vibrant blue flowers. This must be the place.

The sound of the water flowing from the fountain into the pool is soothing, and it draws us in. As we get closer to the pool we can see that there is a wide stone walkway between the palm trees and the pool so people can walk around it. And there are benches every few yards.

The park seems to be deserted. As we pass by the pool,

we can see that the blue flowers growing in the water are lotuses.

Sitting on a bench overlooking the pool is a woman. She is dressed in a short white linen sleeveless tunic that goes up over one shoulder. Around her waist is a green sash. Around her upper right arm is a gold band studded with green stones. She wears large gold hoop earrings. Her skin is deeply tanned, like she has spent much time in the sun.

"Welcome," she says as we approach. "Come and sit with me." We sit on either side of her. "I come here often," she says. "It's very familiar: the gardens, the palm trees, the lotus blossoms. The smells bring back memories of my childhood." I breathe in deeply. The air is warm and dry, and I can smell the sweet scent of the flowers. It stirs vague memories of a trip Margaret and I took to the Middle East.

"What was your childhood like?" she asks. "I was the oldest child in my family, with two younger brothers. My name is Miriam, and my younger brothers are Aaron and Moses."

Miriam! I try to imagine what it would be like to have Moses as a kid brother.

"I grew up as a slave," she says, "so life was hard. But we had our moments. My parents were very loving, but they were usually so tired when they came home that

I took care of them more than they took care of me. I used to sing for them to cheer them up. And I sang for Moses all the time when he was a baby—after we got him back. Mother put him in a basket in the river when he was a baby, but when Pharaoh's daughter found him, she adopted him. I was very proud that it was I who arranged for Mother to be the one to nurse Moses and take care of him until he was weaned. Truth be told, it was I who kept the family together in those early years. I took care of the house. I was also the one who took care of Aaron when he was little. And the time when Mother took care of Moses, before he went to live in the palace, that was a special time for our family because we were all together and Mother did not have to labor in the hot sun."

Miriam sits silently for a few moments. She seems to be thinking. "I was the older sister, the one everyone could depend on. It was a role I loved. It gave me great satisfaction to take care of everyone. But then later, after Moses came back from exile and took all of us out of Egypt, everything changed. I felt like I'd lost my place in the family, and it made me unhappy. I guess some people just have to learn their lessons the hard way, and I'm one of them. But you don't have to. You can learn from my mistakes," she says with intensity. *"Don't let comparison rob you of your joy."*

Let God Be the Judge

"It's difficult when you go from being a leader that others admire to being in the background. All my life I had been a leader. Aaron was a people pleaser that other people could sway this way and that. And Moses had been gone a long time before he returned to lead us out of Egypt. When he first returned, I was ecstatic. God had finally answered our prayers. We were free. And the day God drowned the Egyptian armies at the bottom of the Red Sea was one of the greatest days of our people. In those moments God spoke to me and I could not contain myself. I felt *compelled* to sing His praises. The words flowed from me, like God Himself had given them to me. And it felt like all the women of Israel joined me and sang along to celebrate God's goodness. It was one of the greatest moments of my life.

"But that sense of joy didn't stay with me all the time. I often felt discontented. I started to compare myself to Moses. I was a prophet too. God had spoken to me. Why was he getting all the attention? It was like a negative seed that had been planted in me that I watered and encouraged to grow in my soul. And that's when my problems began. If you compare yourself to others, the same kinds of problems will occur for you."

"Comparison Makes You Delight in Finding Fault in Others"

"As I compared myself to my younger brother and found myself falling short, it ate at me. Comparison turned into jealousy. Jealously led to discontentment. That fueled my anger and made my attitude even more negative until I became bitter.

"So I began looking for things to criticize my brother for. But Moses's time in exile had humbled him. Whatever pride he'd once possessed was gone. He had become soft-spoken and gentle. And it seemed that whatever God asked him to do, he did.

"I'm ashamed to say that when I couldn't find anything legitimate to criticize in him, I started grasping at straws. The best I could come up with was to say something spiteful about his wife not being an Israelite, because she was from Cush. When you see yourself in a bad light, you go out of your way to find fault in others."

"Comparison Drives You to Seek Positive Attention for Yourself"

"Comparing ourselves to others is a no-win activity. There are always people less talented or favored than us. When we compare ourselves to them, we feel superior. There are also people more talented and blessed than us. When we compare ourselves to them, we feel inferior. In either case the comparison makes us seek affirmation and attention from others.

"God blessed me with musical ability. He also made me a prophet. But when I compared myself to Moses, that didn't seem like enough. I wanted to be recognized. So I started to complain to my other brother, Aaron. I pulled him into my discontentment. That did not please God, so He struck me with leprosy."

"Comparison Damages Your Relationship with Others"

"Even after I was so petty and negative about Moses, he still interceded with God for me. That just made me feel worse. He was in the right while I was clearly in the wrong, yet he still loved me and begged God to heal me, which God did. But the truth is that even though Moses still loved me, I think he always wondered after that if he could trust me fully. I always regretted that."

"Comparison Undermines Your Usefulness to God"

"The bottom line is that when you long for the gifts, favor, position, or opportunities of someone else, it distracts you from the gifts, favor, position, and opportunities that God has given *you*. God wanted to use me, but I was so distracted from what I could do that I never fully reached my potential. And jealousy killed my joy. Don't fall into that trap. Don't allow that to happen to you."

Life Lessons from Miriam

Miriam's recollection of that time seemed to cloud her expression. Perhaps from the perspective of heaven it was painful for her to remember the foolishness and shortsightedness she displayed when she was on earth. If that was the case, the moment seems to have passed, because she smiles at us, the worry lines in her face transforming into laugh lines.

"My loss is your gain," she says, patting us each on the arm in turn. "Here are four things you can learn from my experience."

"Just Because You Are Capable Doesn't Mean You Are Called"

"God gives many skills and talents. He gives them to every human being into which He breathes life. Some of those talents are greater, some lesser. Some tap into your passion; some don't. Some lead you straight to your purpose;

others lead you astray. You have to make choices. Just because you see something you *could* do does not automatically mean it is something you *should* do. Don't let the desire to do something you could do well prevent you from doing what's really best."

"You Should Compare Yourself to Only One Person"

"For much of my life I compared myself to other people. I compared myself to my mother. I compared myself to the other girls who lived near my home. I compared myself to other young women in the community. And of course I also compared myself to my brothers. Every one of those comparisons was wrong.

"Whom should I have compared myself to? Me. The only worthy comparison people can make is between who they are and who God created them to be. There are two fantastic things about that. First, God doesn't condemn us when we fall short. And second, He has given us the tools to actually become that person. We simply need to keep working at it to get there."

"You Must Try to Find Contentment in the Role God Has Given You"

"When I spoke out against Moses with Aaron, it was because I felt I wasn't getting enough credit for my role as one of Israel's leaders. When God rebuked me, His words exposed my jealousy. God said,

> Listen carefully to what I'm telling you.
> If there is a prophet of GOD among you,
> I make myself known to him in visions,
> I speak to him in dreams.
> But I don't do it that way with my servant Moses;
> he has the run of my entire house;
> I speak to him intimately, in person,
> in plain talk without riddles:
> He ponders the very form of GOD.
> So why did you show no reverence or respect
> in speaking against my servant, against Moses?[24]

"Moses had what I wanted. God *did* speak to me in dreams. But I wanted the intimacy God had given my brother.

"You know what role God has given you. You know your gifts—or at least I hope you do. Be content with those and make the most of them. Don't go to your grave wishing you were someone else."

"You Can Change a Bad Attitude by Cultivating Gratitude"

"I learned my lesson in Hazeroth. After being struck with leprosy, I had seven days in quarantine outside of the camp to think about what I had done. And I made the determination that I would never again allow jealousy to overtake me. Whenever I was tempted, I didn't allow myself to start comparing myself to others. Instead I made an inventory of all the wonderful things God was doing in my life and of all the things He had given me.

"You know, that's why God kept telling His people to remember what He'd done for them. It's why He asked our descendants to remember the story of me, my brothers, and all the people God delivered out of Egypt. He knew that if we remembered, we would be grateful. And when you're grateful, you become someone God is capable of using for mankind's benefit and for God's glory."

The Prayer of Miriam

As we listen to Miriam, I am reminded that life's greatest lessons are taught to us by our failures and losses. Success has its own lessons, but often they are difficult to see.

Failure's lessons are much easier to find—as long as we have courage enough to look for them.

"God has been so kind to me," says Miriam, "that I would like to pray for you.

"Merciful Heavenly Father,

"You formed each of us in our mothers' wombs, and You knew even before we were born what You made us capable of. You know what my friends can do. You know what they will do. And You are not disappointed with them. Teach them not to compare themselves to anyone else. Release them from any past pains or shortcomings, as You did with me. Teach them to live for Your glory, and keep themselves focused entirely upon You. Amen."

When we open our eyes, Miriam is silent. When she realizes we are watching her, she smiles.

Leadership Lessons from Miriam

"Your next appointment is with someone very special. She is already waiting for you up on the next level of the city. If you look at the houses over on that side of the park," she says, pointing to the side opposite the street where we entered, "you will find a staircase. Go up it, and you will find her there."

Miriam stands. "You are welcome to sit here as long as you like, but I must go. Good-bye." She turns away and walks back in the direction from which we came. Now that we're not focused on her, we can simply sit and enjoy the view and the peaceful atmosphere. We also take time to think about the leadership lessons we can learn from Miriam's experience.

1. Recognize That All Leaders Are Not Created Equal

We live in a culture where people say they value fairness. But have you ever noticed that people are more vocal when asking others to raise them up and less vocal about how they should make personal sacrifices to help those who are less privileged than they are? I guess what that really means is that they want fairness most when it is to their advantage.

But God never promised to be fair with us. That's actually a good thing, since all of us fall short of the glory of God and deserve to be condemned. Instead God offers us grace. And He gives us a chance to make a difference with whatever He *has* given us.

The parable of the talents says some people have five talents, others two, and some one. God does not give gifts equally. We need to respect that. God chose to meet with Moses face-to-face and to speak directly to him—and not to the other prophets. For Moses that was a great privilege—and a weighty responsibility.

Whatever gifts God has given you are a privilege and a responsibility. Treat them accordingly. And don't worry about whether they are more or less than another leader's. That's God's business, not yours. He's not comparing you to them, so neither should you.

2. Understand That Leadership Is a Privilege and a Trust

Talented people, especially talented leaders, can begin to think of their role or position as a right. That is never the case. If you have been given a leadership role, God has given it to you for the sake of others, not for yourself. Miriam lost sight of that for a time. God used her mightily when Moses was a baby. God used her again to lead others in worshipping God. At those times she acted selflessly. But when she became jealous, she was thinking of herself, not others.

Whatever influence you possess, use it wisely. Hold

your leadership role loosely. It's not yours for your benefit. It's a trust God has given you to serve others. Serve them well.

3. Learn to Celebrate Other Leaders' Successes

Miriam had a difficult time celebrating Moses's lofty role in God's plan for His people, but she was not the only one prone to jealousy. Immediately before the incident in which Miriam was struck with leprosy, God's Spirit came down on some of the elders around the tent of meeting, who began prophesying. When two other men who had stayed in the camp also began prophesying, it upset some of the people, including Joshua. Scripture says,

> Joshua son of Nun, who had been Moses's right-hand man since his youth, said, "Moses, master! Stop them!"
>
> But Moses said, "Are you jealous for me? Would that all GOD's people were prophets. Would that GOD would put his Spirit on all of them."[25]

As leaders we are often naturally competitive. We like winning. But that doesn't give us permission to tear others down. William Penn said, "The jealous are troublesome to others, but a torment to themselves." Try to remember that all leaders serving God are on the same team. When others are successful, celebrate. Their success points to God's worthiness, not your shortcomings.

It takes a secure person to celebrate when others win. It takes a grateful person to be content with whom God has made him or her to be. Miriam is a good reminder of that. Her change of heart is a great lesson to us.

Woman to Woman

What I find fascinating about Miriam is that she became envious in spite of all the ways God had already used her. God had chosen Miriam for wonderful roles—from protector of her baby brother on the Nile River to prophetess singing praises to God after all the Israelites crossed the Red Sea in their escape from Egypt. She was brave, dedicated, and determined.

Miriam did amazing things—until she lost her focus on what God had called her to, and started to focus on what Moses got to do. It took leprosy to snap her out of her wrong perspective. I guess

(*Continued*)

you could say that was God's attitude improvement plan for Miriam! But she did finally learn the lesson. It's a lesson that God desires all of us to learn: God has a special purpose and plan for every woman.

We are all given a unique purpose by God. You and I must stay disciplined and focused on this plan for us individually, and not let our thoughts stray to the plans God has for others. Miriam's story reminds me that I need to look to God, not others, for my worth and purpose.

—Trish Throckmorton

Questions for Reflection or Discussion

To learn more about Miriam, read Exodus 2:7–8 and 15: 20–21, Numbers 12:1 and 20:1-16, 1 Chronicles 6:3, and Micah 6:4.

1. Why do you think Miriam started comparing herself to Moses and getting angry?
2. When you were growing up, did you often get compared to someone else? How did it make you feel?
3. Are you naturally more inclined to compare yourself to people who are more talented than you, thus making yourself feel inadequate, or to people less talented in an attempt to validate yourself?
4. When you don't feel like you're getting proper recognition for your skills or contributions, how do you respond?
5. When do you find it easy to celebrate the successes of others, and when do you find it difficult? Explain why.
6. Can you think of a time when you missed a great opportunity because, instead of appreciating the gifts and skills you had, you were focused on wanting to do something you were less suited for? Explain.
7. What God-given skill or ability do you possess that you take for granted? How can you better use it to serve others and glorify God?

MARY

Don't Miss Your Moment with God

We walk past the circular pond and dozens of beautiful flower beds, and we head for the middle of the far side of the park. There between two houses is a staircase, just as Miriam said there would be. Once again I am surprised, because the stairs are made of yet another kind of stone. This time it is a clear vivid green. It looks like emerald. Not only the stair treads and risers are made of it, but also the walls—like the entire passageway has been cut into a giant piece of emerald.

We step onto the staircase and begin climbing. As we move up slowly, I grasp the handrail that has been carved into the stone along the wall. I run my hand along it and discover that it's perfectly smooth. I can't detect a single joint, crack, or flaw.

We climb quite a long time, and my knees begin to ache. I'm surprised that there are no obvious stopping points or landings along the way where we can rest. I guess the new bodies people receive in heaven don't fatigue the way ours do, and the stairway is built for them. I stop to catch my breath more than once.

When we arrive at the top of the stairway, we find ourselves on a different kind of street from the one at the level below. Where the last street was long, level, and perfectly straight, this one is narrow and winding. To the left the street slopes downward. In the other direction it slopes gently upward. We can't see too far in either direction because the street curves.

On the previous level, there was space between the buildings that fronted the road, and many had yards or gardens in front of them. This street looks nothing like that. The fronts of the buildings are right on the narrow road, and they are attached to one another so that they have the feel of one long continuous building. It reminds me of the streets in the Old City of Jerusalem.

People pass by on the street in both directions. They seem to be purposeful, but not hurried. Standing in the middle of the street, like a stone in a river of rushing water, is a small woman dressed in pale blue. Her long cloak is tied at the waist with a white sash. Her head covering seems to be made of the same white fabric.

Everyone seems careful not to run into her. Some men

tip their hats. Other people bow. All of them, it seems, acknowledge her in some way. I wonder who commands this kind of respect and attention.

Although she returns people's greetings, the focus of her gaze is clearly on us. When we make eye contact with her, she smiles and beckons us with her hand.

"Hello, my friends," she says as we approach. "Let's walk together."

The woman leads us up the curved street for maybe a hundred yards, until we see a very small passage to the left. We take it and immediately we are out of the main flow of people. The pathway we're on is sloped upward and winds to and fro.

"This is better," she says as we walk slowly together. "People are always wanting to greet me or talk to me, but I don't think we'll be interrupted quite as much here."

"Who are you?" I ask.

"Mary," she answers. "Jesus's mother."

No wonder, I think. That's why everyone is so deferential to her. She gave birth to and took care of the Savior of the world, God Himself in human flesh.

"There are times in the life of every person," Mary says as we walk slowly, "when God reveals Himself and asks that we do something. That is a special God moment, so take heed: *Don't miss your moment with God.*"

In the Moment

"That special moment occurred for me when the angel Gabriel appeared to me. Believe me, it came as a total surprise to me. I was an ordinary girl. I grew up in an ordinary home with two ordinary parents. It's true that I loved God and wanted to please Him, but I don't think I was any different from most other people in Israel.

"It was a very special time for me." Mary pauses as she seems to recall the days of her youth. "I had just entered my engagement period with Joseph. I was so excited that we would soon be married. Joseph was a kind man, and he had a good trade, so I knew he would provide for us. I was looking forward to setting up a household in Nazareth with him, and my mother was helping me with the preparations. Our new life together was about to begin, and I hoped that we would soon have a house full of children.

"I almost fainted when Gabriel appeared to me. I could tell he wasn't an ordinary man. On top of that, this was his greeting to me:

> Good morning!
> You're beautiful with God's beauty,
> Beautiful inside and out!
> God be with you.[26]

"I could tell by the words he used and by the way he said them that he was about to say something important to me, so I held my breath in anticipation. When he said, 'You will become pregnant and give birth to a son and call his name Jesus,'[27] I was confused because I was a virgin. I remember thinking,

> "What will my friends and family think? They will believe that Joseph and I slept together before being married.

> "What will Joseph think? He will believe I've been unfaithful and slept with another man. He may reject me forever.

> "What will the religious authorities think? They may drag me out into the street and condemn me to death by stoning!

"Then when he said my child would be called the Son of God, my head started spinning. I was terrified.

"In that moment I felt like time stopped. I could feel the weight of the decision I needed to make, and I could tell that it was in my power to say no if I wanted to. More questions rushed into my head: Would I be capable of rising to this challenge? What would it cost me personally? What would this different future look like? What if I failed? What if I was crazy and this message wasn't really from God?

"Doubts filled my mind. I could think of dozens of reasons to say no to God. But my heart told me to say yes because I loved Him. So in spite of my fears, my doubts, my questions about the future, I said yes. I didn't know how things would turn out, but I put myself into the hands of God anyway because I trusted Him."

The Crucible

I try to imagine what it must have been like to be a young teenage girl living in a culture where women had no voice, and where being unmarried and pregnant was a crime punishable by death. All the odds were against her, yet she said yes. That moment was a crucible that made clear what her relationship with God was. Her encounter had characteristics that I believe can teach us about God moments:

- ***They are initiated by God, not us.*** Mary didn't ask for the experience she received. Nor could she have created it on her own. Only God could do it. That's always true.

- *They are unanticipated.* Not only did Mary not ask for the experience, she was totally surprised by it. This is also always true of these God moments.

- *They are connected to God's favor.* It was a great privilege for Mary to be chosen for this task. It's a privilege *any* time God chooses one of us to help fulfill His purpose.

- *They offer insights from God.* Gabriel told Mary things about her future that she could not know. Encounters with God give us glimpses of understanding.

- *They are not understood.* It's ironic, but even though God reveals things to us, we usually don't know what they mean. This was the case even for the disciples, who heard things from Jesus Himself, yet didn't get it.

- *They are supernatural.* Mary's moment was dramatic because God sent an angel to speak to her. Our encounters with God may not include angels, but that doesn't make them any less supernatural.

- *They require us to say yes.* When God invites us into what He's doing, He is giving us a chance to partner with Him. But we must say yes to the partnership.

- **They change your life and the lives of others.**
  When God gives us an invitation and we choose to
  accept it, nothing in our lives will ever be the same
  again. Neither will the lives of the other people
  affected by our decision.

God moments always put us off balance. They overwhelm us. They disrupt our lives. They make us uncomfortable. How many times have I been certain God was speaking to me, yet didn't say yes to Him? Whenever we are willing to trust God and say yes to Him, our lives take on new meaning and direction. I don't want to miss that.

Life Lessons from Mary

I wonder what Mary's life would have been like if she had said no to God instead of saying, "I'm the Lord's maid, ready to serve. Let it be with me just as you say."[28] Would Jesus have been born to another young woman in Nazareth? Would He still have been a carpenter? Would Mary have still recognized that Jesus was the Son of God? There's no way to know.

My mind is racing, but my attention is brought back to Mary as she begins to speak once more.

"You Were Created to Be a Vessel for the Impossible"

"You are, I'm afraid, at a little bit of a disadvantage because you live in a time when people value facts more than they do truth. I think that causes many people to misunderstand God and what He desires for His people. We were not created for mundane lives. We were created to be extraordinary. We are God's instruments of impossibility.

"What may be an impossibility for us is merely an opportunity for God. Miracles happen when our willingness to serve God intersects with His revealed plan. Knowing that should change your approach to every year, every day, every minute that you live."

"When Your Moment Comes, Say Yes and Let God Figure Out the Rest"

"If you want God to do the impossible in your life, you cannot allow fear to cloud your view of God and what He can do. Your hope must weigh more than your questions. Your trust must be greater than your doubt.

"When God invites you to do something for Him, don't try to figure out how God will fulfill His purpose. It is a waste of time. The solution is God's problem. Besides,

God loves to surprise us. He's creative. He does things we can't imagine in our wildest dreams. Say yes, and then watch how He works it all out."

"If You've Already Missed One God Moment, Be Ready for the Next One"

"Maybe you've heard from God, as I did, but you didn't say yes. Maybe you knew you should do something, yet you talked yourself out of it. Or you felt a challenge from God to act, but you were too afraid or lazy to follow through. I believe all of us have God moments when we fall short of God's invitation.

"If that is true for you, let it go. God is merciful and kind. Don't waste your energy looking backward. Don't get bogged down in regret. Instead look forward. Make yourself ready for the next opportunity, for almost certainly God will give you another one. Ask God to make it clear to you when He next speaks so that you recognize the moment for what it is. And resolve to say yes, no matter how many questions or doubts you may have."

"Your Yes Will Open the Door for God's Best If You Let It"

"You will never regret saying yes to God. It's true that when God gives us an opportunity to say yes to Him, we can see all the reasons to say no. All those negative ideas can be overwhelming. But you need to understand something: the reasons to say yes are usually hidden. There are more reasons to say yes than to say no, but you can't see them at that time. Only after we say yes are we able to see them.

"We just need to have faith that God's best always comes after we are obedient to Him. And what's really fantastic is that obedience and a willingness to say yes can become the hallmark of your life."

Those words make a strong impression on us. When I think about how Mary had to make this big decision when she was only a girl, it causes me to marvel. But when you look at her later in her life, you see that same attitude. It comes out in the story of the wedding banquet in Cana. Mary asks Jesus to do something when the guests run out of wine, but Jesus is reluctant to act because it is not His time. Mary solves the problem by telling the servants, "Whatever he tells you, do it."[29] Of course she would say that. That phrase could be the theme of her life. Appreciating Mary's faith and seeing the servants filling several large vessels with water, Jesus turns the water into wine. Once again Mary's trust in God helped her seize the moment.

The Prayer of Mary

When Mary was talking to us, her faith was so deep and her quiet confidence so strong that she almost seemed physically larger than she actually is. Now that she's quiet, she seems smaller again and rather ordinary. But everything changes again when she starts to pray as we continue to walk:

"My Faithful Lord and Master,

"I boldly request that You speak to these dear servants of Yours. Ask big things of them. Make them uncomfortable. Stretch them in ways that they have no idea You can. And give them the will, the heart, and the faith to say a wholehearted yes to You whenever You ask. May their obedience change not only them, but the world. Amen."

The power and confidence of her words are amazing— but not surprising. How could it be otherwise? Her journey with Jesus began with a yes to God, and then she was an eyewitness to nearly everything He did.

Moments after she finishes the prayer, we come to the end of the narrow street we've been walking on and arrive at an intersection with another road. The pathway we've been on is winding, and it turned back and forth so many times that I've lost all sense of direction. I'm surprised to see that we are at the edge of a forest.

"Walk this way into the woods," says Mary, indicating that we go to the left. "You'll find the next person who wants to meet with you there."

Leadership Lessons from Mary

We watch as Mary walks away in the other direction. Again she looks small and ordinary. If we hadn't met her and heard her speak, we would have little idea how strong and significant a person she is. She is a great reminder that leaders come in all shapes and sizes. Some are like Saul: they impress us, they are physically imposing, and they possess a commanding presence when they walk into a room. Others are like Mary, whose ordinary appearance hides a deep, quiet strength.

Mary's example reminds me of some important truths about leadership. If you want to lead well, you must...

1. Stay Connected to God

Mary was a candidate for God's blessing because she was close to God. And during her lifetime, she stayed close to God—literally, as she raised Jesus. But she wasn't passive as she cared for Him. Luke says that when extraordinary things happened, Mary treasured them in her heart and pondered them.[30]

No matter how much or how little natural leadership talent God has given you, you cannot go wrong by staying connected to God. The ability to know and follow His direction always has much greater value than any human skill.

2. Stay Connected to Your Purpose

From the time before Jesus was even conceived, Mary knew her purpose. It was her purpose to bear, raise, nurture, and care for the Son of God. Raising any child isn't easy. Having responsibility for Jesus must have weighed upon Mary heavily. But she bore it with grace, and she was faithful to the end.

When you have doubts, face difficulties, or need to make tough decisions, don't depart from your purpose. If you know why God has put you on earth, use that knowledge as a touchstone. If you don't know your purpose, ask God to reveal it. Meanwhile, use whatever you *do* know to help you.

3. Stay Connected to People Who Encourage You

Soon after Mary learned that God was going to use her to do something extraordinary but very difficult, what did she do? She went to spend time with her cousin Elizabeth, with whom she was close. Elizabeth encouraged her and helped her get ready for what lay ahead.

I believe that Jesus's actions show that He also recognized the importance of encouragement to Mary. As He was dying on the cross, He asked His disciple John to take His place caring for Mary—and who better than John, the disciple Jesus loved, to care for the mother Jesus loved? The more difficult the circumstances, the more we need and benefit from the encouragement of others.

4. Stay Connected to the Bigger Picture

There must have been many times when Mary wondered what was going on and what God was doing, just as she did that first day when Gabriel came to speak with her. She knew she was raising God's Son, but she could not have known that He was preparing to sacrifice Himself for the world's sin. As she watched Him dying on the cross, she once again had to trust God and rely on her faith in Him for the bigger picture.

That's a good reminder for us as leaders. God always has the bigger picture in mind. We can trust Him. The more we remember that, the better we can serve Him when we don't understand what we may be dealing with.

*　　*　　*

Mary is an inspiration. She didn't miss that first God moment, and I have a feeling she experienced many others. Her actions make me want to seek God's favor, rely on His direction, and trust Him when the time comes.

Woman to Woman

What I admire most about Mary, the mother of Jesus, is her humble spirit in accepting such a precious gift. This was something far beyond her understanding, yet she gracefully took on the biggest job anyone could ever have. This was despite the fear she must have felt about what people would think of her, and the real possibility of being stoned to death for becoming pregnant before marriage. I am impressed with her strength and courage, both emotionally and physically. Emotionally, she withstood the gossip that would flood through her town. Physically, she traveled to Bethlehem while very pregnant, and even fled to Egypt to escape Herod soon after the baby was born.

Mary must have struggled with anxiety about an unknown future, yet she had faith that God's plan for her life was far better than her own. Although I am

(*Continued*)

sure that at times it was hard to trust that the Lord's way was right, she was obedient to Him. I can only imagine the joy she felt as she watched Jesus grow and change people's lives with His miracles and teaching. I'm sure there was many a day when she thought, "What if I had said no?" Faith is believing in things that are unseen, and what character in the Bible models that better than the mother of Jesus?

The lesson to be learned from Mary is to wholeheartedly trust the Lord. God has a much bigger plan for my life than I have for myself. I may tend to become nervous about the future, but that's where my faith, courage, and strength need to come in to keep me moving forward. Without the help of the Lord, I might crumble and fail, but when God is in the picture, I can rise above the obstacles of anxiety and fear. It just takes a yes.

I will forever picture Mary as a hero to all women, who took on a fantastic yet frightening challenge, one that changed the world. My goal in life is to have the strength and courage that Mary had to say yes. If I say yes to God and let Him work through me, I too can change this world for His glory.

—Elizabeth Miller

Questions for Reflection or Discussion

To learn more about Mary, read Matthew 1:18–2:23, 13: 53–57, 27:55–61, and 28:1–10, Luke 1:26–2:29, John 19: 24–27, and Acts 1:14.

1. If you had found yourself in Mary's situation, where you believed God was asking you to do something that could turn your entire life upside down, how do you think you would have reacted?

2. Are you naturally more of a dreamer, who hopes for the impossible, or a skeptic, who is more pragmatic? How does that affect your relationship with God?

3. When do you find it difficult to trust God and when do you find it easy?

4. What do you do to try to stay connected to God? How well is it currently working for you?

5. Have you ever experienced a moment where you believe God invited you to do something for Him, but you did not say yes? If so, how has that affected your life?

6. How can a person make him- or herself a candidate for a God moment?

7. If in the future God invites you to do something uncomfortable or seemingly impossible for Him, what will you do to process that decision?

MARTHA

*When Jesus Is in the House, Give Him
Your Full Attention*

We walk along the narrow road into the forest. The area is green and lush. The trees, which are spaced widely, tower over us. Their rough bark is brown and gray. I have to look up to see any branches. The canopy of the trees is so high that it's hard to tell what kind of trees they are, but I think they may be conifers of some type.

Except for the pathway we walk on, the ground is covered with a carpet of thick, tufty grass. It looks soft and inviting. I'd love to take off my shoes and walk in it. Scattered here and there over the forest floor are purple and white wildflowers.

The path we walk on is made of jet-black square stones laid out in a diamond pattern. The grass stretching out on either side is beautifully uneven and textured with little mounds, but the path is smooth and precisely laid out.

Before long we begin to see houses in among the trees of the forest. They appear to be comfortably distant from one another, and the structures, though made of gold, take many different forms architecturally. Some are cabins made of golden logs. Others are huts. A few look like they could have been plucked out of the American suburbs. Each has a path or stepping stones leading from the road we walk up to the front door.

Just as we start to hesitate and wonder if we are supposed to walk up to one of these buildings, we hear a woman's voice calling, "Hello. Come this way. I'm over here."

We look and see a woman dressed in orange about thirty yards away, standing in front of a small building. She is waving at us and smiling.

We walk just a bit longer along the narrow road, then take the pathway on the right that leads to the building where she's standing. Its walls are in the shape of fitted stones, and the roof is flat. It reminds me of buildings I once saw in a scale model of an ancient Israelite town. It looks a bit odd sitting by itself surrounded by thick grass between the trees.

"Come, come," the woman says. "I have things to discuss with you." As we arrive she says, "Sit. Please sit." She is sitting on a large black stone. We sit on stones near her. "Here," she says, handing each of us a crystal goblet, "I bet you're thirsty. Why don't you rest a moment?" I take a drink. The only way I can describe it is as the best drink of water I've ever had. I relax, and look at the grass close by.

"Go ahead," she says.

She's taken me off guard. "Go ahead and what?" I ask.

"Go ahead and walk in the grass. Take off your shoes. It's all right. I'll take mine off too."

You and I look at each other. Why not? As the woman in orange removes her sandals, we take off our shoes. As I take my first step in the grass it's exactly as I expected it to be—cool and soft and wonderful. I wiggle and flex my toes, and I feel any fatigue in my legs from the walking we've done vanishing—it's flowing from me like water soaking into the turf.

"Isn't it marvelous?" says the woman in orange as she walks through the grass. "It's one of the reasons I live here. I love walking in the grass, picking the wildflowers, or simply sitting and listening to the wind move the branches of the trees."

I like this woman. She knows how to stop and smell the roses—or rather the wildflowers.

"Who are you?" I ask her.

"I'm Martha," she says, "the sister of Mary and Lazarus."

Slow Down!

Martha—I never would have guessed it. Because of the way Martha interacted with Jesus, I see her as a type A personality—a doer who's not afraid to tell others what to think and do. Martha never appeared to hold back when interacting with Jesus. When He arrived at Bethany after Lazarus had already died, Martha said to Him, "Master, if you'd been here, my brother wouldn't have died. Even now, I know that whatever you ask God he will give you."[31]

In another encounter with Jesus, when He visited the home of Lazarus, Martha worked in the kitchen, preparing the food and getting everything ready for her guests while her sister Mary simply sat with Jesus, listening to Him. Martha resented that and told Jesus so. She said, "Master, don't you care that my sister has abandoned the kitchen to me? Tell her to lend me a hand."[32]

I'm so surprised that I find myself asking, "How did someone so pragmatic and focused on doing become so relaxed?"

"That's easy," Martha answers. "I listened to Jesus. I missed it at first, but after seeing my sister pour oil on

Jesus's feet and just love Him, it finally became clear to me: *When Jesus is in the house, give Him your full attention.*"

"I Didn't Know How to Slow Down"

"Look, when Jesus arrived at my home that day, I didn't understand that there are not very many Jesus moments in life. That was true for me, and in those days Jesus was actually present in body in my house. It's also true for you. Jesus is always with us through the power of the Holy Spirit, but even devout people who love God, pray, serve faithfully, worship, and read Scripture don't have many of these moments. When Jesus was in the house on that day, my sister Mary recognized not to miss the moment, but I didn't."

"I Thought Duty Was More Important than Devotion"

"My whole life I was very aware of my responsibilities. As the oldest sister, I was expected to take care of my siblings. My mother expected it. After she died, I stepped into her role completely. I had always been willing to do my duty and took pride in it. But that's not what Jesus wanted from me. I offered duty. He wanted devotion. It wasn't clear then, but it is now:

Duty	Devotion
Welcomes Jesus	Welcomes Jesus
Gets distracted	Focuses on Jesus
Misreads Jesus	Sits at the feet of Jesus and listens
Tries to impress Him through work	Sits at the feet of Jesus and listens
Feels superior	Sits at the feet of Jesus and listens
Gets worked up over nothing	Sits at the feet of Jesus and listens
Becomes resentful	Sits at the feet of Jesus and listens
Does everything but the main thing	Sits at the feet of Jesus and listens

"People with my personality tend to fall into duty mode. We get to work. Jesus wants us to slow down and spend time with Him."

"I Got Caught Up Preparing for Jesus Instead of Preparing Myself for Jesus"

"When we host others, we want to prepare things just so. We want our guests to be comfortable and taken care of. There's nothing wrong with that. But we need to remember something: Jesus isn't our guest. He's our Savior!

"I wanted to please Jesus. I welcomed Him into the house, but then all the preparations that had to be made took all of my attention. Jesus entered the room, and I left the room to go into the kitchen. It's sometimes easier to serve Jesus than to stay with Jesus."

"I Got Worked Up Over Unimportant Things Instead of Focusing on the Main Thing"

"There's a difference between letting Jesus into your life and actually being with Him and connecting with Him. I love Jesus, and I loved Him back then. But He made me uncomfortable. Mary's uninhibited love for Him made me uncomfortable too. I had to learn how to become comfortable with my discomfort so that Jesus could change me.

"Truth be told, many people who believe in Jesus find it difficult to spend time with Him. He makes them uncomfortable, and they don't know what to do with that. If you haven't discovered how to simply *be* with Jesus, then it's time you learn."

Life Lessons from Martha

What a pleasant surprise Martha is. I think many people have given her a bad rap. Her mistake is recorded in Scripture for everyone to remember. Not recorded is what she learned from it. When Jesus visited, her intentions were good. She was practical, hospitable, and willing to serve. In comparison to her devoted and extravagant sister Mary, she may have come off as pushy and harsh. She simply needed to learn how to interact with Jesus in the best way.

We continue to walk among the trees in the soft grass. I think even a hard charger like me could learn to enjoy such a place.

"My hope," says Martha, "is that you can learn some things from my life."

"When Jesus Shows Up, Don't Get Busy—Stop What You're Doing"

"It doesn't matter where you are or what you're doing: when Jesus is in the house, focus on Him. There is no other appropriate way to respond. When Judas fussed at Mary for pouring expensive oil on Jesus's feet, our Lord said, 'You always have the poor with you. You don't always have me.'[33] Jesus could have also said, 'There will always be work for you to do, but I won't always be here in the house with you.'

"When Jesus shows up, don't go do something else. Don't go into the kitchen or workroom. Don't get busy. Stop and hang with Jesus. That's why He is there with you."

"When Jesus Shows Up, Don't Focus on Serving—Focus on Connecting"

"When my sister Mary sat at Jesus's feet, broke the bottle of nard, poured it on Jesus's feet, and then dried His feet with her hair, she wasn't doing it to make His feet clean. It was to give Jesus her entire attention and show Him how much she loved Him.

"I learned this lesson by watching my little sister. That's not easy. I was always the one setting the example. This time she set the example for me. And it's a lesson I learned well."

"When Jesus Shows Up, Don't Try to Take Control—Get on His Agenda"

"I must admit, I enjoyed being in charge. It made me feel good. I like getting things done. I like the feeling of accomplishing things. Maybe you do too. When you're hosting, serving, or doing, you feel like you are in control. However, when you sit at Jesus's feet, He is in control. That can be difficult.

"I look back now and realize I should have learned this lesson when Jesus let Lazarus die and then brought him back to life. When Jesus arrived in Bethany, I scolded Him for not coming sooner. All I could think about was myself and what I wanted. I loved my brother. But Jesus was following God's agenda. He saw a bigger picture. He always does. I missed that. But I learned the lesson the next time. Don't you miss it."

"When Jesus Shows Up, Don't Try to Do Something for Him—Just Be with Him"

"When Jesus is in the house, it's not about what I'm doing for Him. It's about what He's doing—no matter what that may be. We don't know when He will show up. We don't know what His agenda will be. We don't know what He is going to want to say or do. We just need to be willing to stop and be with Him. When we do that, we find out things about Him and about ourselves."

The Prayer of Martha

We've been so focused on Martha and listening to her so intently that I didn't realize we had arrived back in front of the small house where we started. And from the look she gives us, I realize that our time with her has come to an end. We are sitting on the grass, preparing to put our shoes back on, when Martha places a hand on each of our heads and starts to pray:

"Gracious and Forgiving God,

*"I am so grateful that You give us opportunities
to change and grow so that we can draw closer to
You and become more like You. Teach my friends
to know with certainty when You are in the house,
and show them how to slow down to Your pace and
connect with You. In the name of Jesus, Amen."*

I look up and smile at Martha. She returns a relaxed and contented smile back to us.

"There is only one more person for you to meet today," says Martha, and my smile disappears, because I realize our time is nearly over. "She will share with you one final truth—perhaps the most important one of all."

We finish putting on our shoes and stand up.

"Go back to the narrow road and continue on in the way you were going when I called to you," says Martha. "Your final mentor will be waiting for you up ahead."

Leadership Lessons from Martha

As we walk back to the road, I'm torn. I want to hear the important truth that will be shared by the next person, but I'm also acutely aware of how little time we have left here. And I want to enjoy every minute of it.

We slow down. As we walk we enjoy the trees, the wildflowers, and the fresh air. We also think about the leadership lessons to be learned from Martha.

1. Don't Let a Bias toward Action Keep You from Stopping to Be with Jesus

Leaders possess a natural bias toward action. The stronger the leadership gifting, the more powerful the penchant for moving things forward, solving problems, and creating momentum. That built-in desire can be a tremendous asset. However, it can also work against you.

Our duties are never more pressing than our need for Jesus. That's true whether we're leaders or not. If we want to live a good life and become more like Christ, we need to spend time with Him. We need to allow Him to show us where we need to change. We need to learn His character so that we can imitate it. We can't do that at high speed. We must slow down and make time for Him.

2. Don't Allow Your Ability to Get a Lot Done Make You Feel Superior to Others

Martha worked hard and got a lot done. Those are good things. But you can tell by the way she talked to Jesus about her sister that she started to think of herself as superior to Mary. That wasn't right. Jesus didn't love

Martha more because of what she got done. Jesus values everyone.

If God has given you a lot of energy or talent or leadership ability, you may appear to others to be more favored by God or to have greater value. It isn't true. God loves you no more than the person who accomplishes nothing for Him. For that reason you should adopt Jesus's attitude toward others. Paul said it this way:

> Think of yourselves the way Christ Jesus thought of himself. He had equal status with God but didn't think so much of himself that he had to cling to the advantages of that status no matter what. Not at all. When the time came, he set aside the privileges of deity and took on the status of a slave, became *human*! Having become human, he stayed human. It was an incredibly humbling process. He didn't claim special privileges. Instead, he lived a selfless, obedient life and then died a selfless, obedient death—and the worst kind of death at that—a crucifixion.[34]

So if you believe you have advantages over others, don't use them. And don't be fooled into thinking you deserve better than others do.

3. If Jesus Shows Up When You're Leading, Follow Where He Leads

It's very easy as leaders for us to get on our own agenda. That's what Martha did. She knew what needed to be done, she had a plan, and she was going to execute it. She had tunnel vision.

If you are a leader who is also a person of faith, you need to be sensitive to the Holy Spirit and learn to pay attention when God shows up. Any time that happens, it is for a reason—God's, not yours. Try to determine what God wants to have happen. Try to figure out what God wants you to do. Maybe He wants you to take bold action. Maybe He wants you to stop others from being rash. Maybe He wants you to model humility. Maybe He wants you to apologize for something you've done. (I'm sorry to say this has happened to me more than once.) Maybe He just wants you to get out of the way.

If Jesus decides to enter the house while you're leading, it's not an accident. He knows what He's doing. Follow Him, and invite others to go with you.

I have to admit, as a highly energetic and action-oriented person who always has an opinion and loves to get things done, it's good for me to think about the wisdom of Martha's words. I love Jesus, and I like to think of myself as someone who is always willing to stop and connect with Him. But Martha's story is a good reminder that you cannot spend too much time with Him. If you are also a person of action, I hope Martha's words have also helped you.

Woman to Woman

I'm intrigued by Martha because, on some level, I can relate to her. Making my guests feel welcome has always been important to me. I love to see them contented and comfortable when we're together. And it's easy when preparing for a special guest to get caught up in the tasks you need to do to welcome them. But I've found that if you really want a guest to feel comfortable once they arrive, you need to give them your full attention.

I believe Martha was trying to make Jesus feel welcome, but her focus was wrong. She was so concerned with what she needed to do for Jesus that she neglected to just be with Him once He was with her. That's where Mary's decision was the right one.

Being with Jesus, giving Him my full attention, is all that He asks of me. Activity does not equal connection. What I love about the lesson that Jesus taught Martha is that it reminds me to focus more on my devotion to Jesus than on my duties. That's truly what makes Him—or any other guest—feel welcome.

—Anita Maxwell

Questions for Reflection or Discussion

To learn more about Martha, read Luke 10:38–42 and John 11:1–44.

1. Whom do you admire more—Martha or her sister Mary? Why?
2. Many people feel that they have too much to do and too little time. How difficult do you find it to get tasks done? Explain.
3. How often do you compare the work you're doing to the work others are getting done? Does it make you feel superior, as Martha did? Or does it make you feel inferior, as Martha was trying to get Mary to feel?
4. Do you find it easy or difficult to stop what you're doing and try to get on God's agenda?
5. What role should duty play when it comes to faith? What role should devotion play?
6. Can you describe a time when you desired clarity about something important to you and received it only when you spent time with God?
7. Many believers find it difficult to just be with Jesus without feeling the need to do something. Is this true for you? If so, how can you change it?

THE SAMARITAN WOMAN

God Will Always Go Out of His Way for You

The narrow road we travel continues to wind through the woods. We pass other houses constructed in a multitude of styles. Soon we can see that the road is taking us toward a cliff wall that rises high above us. The craggy stone face is gray with patches of deep red and brown.

The road we walk looks like it simply stops at the bottom of the cliff, but when we get there, we can see that among the rocks on the left there is a hidden path that slopes upward.

We take the path and start climbing. Before long the path switches back and climbs in the other direction. As we ascend we look down and see the zigzag pattern of the pathway below us. It doesn't take long for us to climb up above the tops of the tall trees, and we can see that the forest is a large rectangle bordered on this side and the left side by cliffs. On the right it's bordered by the city. We can't see what's on the far side opposite us.

After we take one of the turns in the switchback, walls on both sides of the path rise up alongside us to a height of about ten feet so that we can no longer see the view. We take the opportunity to look more closely at the stone that surrounds us. Most of it is gray and pink with an occasional streak of green. Every now and then I see clumps of red, first the size of a walnut, then a softball, growing to the size of a car. The higher we climb, the more red we see.

Just as I feel my legs are about to give out and I'm ready to stop and take a rest, we turn a corner and the path goes in a new direction—away from the forest and directly toward the cliff. We walk up a short staircase made entirely of the red stone that has been polished smooth, and we find ourselves on the shore of a gorgeous lake. It reminds me of Lake Como in Italy. The water, which is a deep blue, is surrounded by craggy mountains. Along the lake's shoreline are beautiful villas.

The road on which we stand seems to be made of the same polished crystalline red stone that the stairway was made of. In the middle of the road ten feet from us is a woman dressed from head to toe in a nondescript brown cloak. Her hair, which peeks out from under her head covering, appears to be almost the same brown. If she were in a crowd instead of standing in the road in front of us, I might not even notice her.

When we look into her face, we can see that she has had a hard life. He features are sharp. Her face is wrinkled. Her brow is furrowed. Hers is the face of one who has seen a lot of pain, a lot of disappointment. But then she smiles at us, and her face transforms. Where we had seen evidence of struggle, we now see joy.

"Come with me," she says. "Our time is short, and I have much to tell you." She doesn't wait, but turns on her heel and begins walking in the other direction along the shoreline of the lake. We quicken our pace so that we catch up with her.

An Unexpected Connection

"The day Jesus came to my village was like any other day. I needed water, but I hated facing the other people who lived there. So I waited until the sun was high overhead before going out with my jar. When I got to the well, I was disappointed to see that someone was there. But I didn't recognize him from the village, and could see by the way he was dressed that he was a Jew, so I was relieved because I knew he would ignore me.

"But he didn't ignore me," she says with great intensity. "He talked to me. And did more than just talk to me. He spoke as though he'd known me my entire life."

"Are you," I stutter, "are you the Samaritan Woman Jesus met at the well in Sychar?"

"Yes, I am," she answers.

"Wow," I respond. "What's your name?"

"That is not for you to know," she answers, "not while you are still to walk the earth. When the apostle John recorded my story, God told him not to write my name."

"But why?" I ask.

"Because my story is your story. It's everyone's story," she answers.

I'm confused, and she must be able to see it in my face, because she goes on to explain.

"My entire life, all I ever wanted was to be loved. I wanted to feel . . . wanted. I think that's true for everyone. We look for acceptance and love in different ways. By the time Jesus came to me and offered to give me living water, I was in my fifties, and life had been hard. I'd been married five times—divorced three times, widowed once, and abandoned once. I'd hoped for a good life, for love, for contentment, yet I never found it. So I did the best I could. And Jesus was right. I had moved into the house of a man in the village without marrying him. It's why the women of the village shunned me. They hated me. And I didn't exactly feel good about myself either.

"It was a surprise when Jesus talked to me. I remember thinking, *If you knew who I was, you wouldn't talk to me.* But then by what He said, He showed that He *did* know me. That was shocking. It was an even greater shock when He told me He was the Messiah. *How could that be? And why would the Messiah be talking to* me? I thought. But nothing could compare to how dumbfounded I was by the way Jesus valued me. He treated me like I was actually worth something. And because He valued me, I had actual value. For the first time in decades, I had hope, and I didn't feel like an outcast.

"Listen to me now, because this is important," she says. "*God will always go out of His way for you.* You can be an outcast, as I was. You can be a king, like David or Solomon. You can be a slave or a celebrity, a common laborer or a professor, a mother or father or sister or son. No matter who you are, *God will go out of His way for you.*"

Life Lessons from the Samaritan Woman

The level of her intensity surprises me. We walk together for a while in silence. I suspect she is letting the words sink in. I look at her and see that she is watching us. Her gaze is intense. As she strides along, I notice something for the first time. As her brown cloak swings, it moves and reveals an inner cloak that is as colorful as the outer cloak is drab. There is more to her than at first meets the eye.

"When Jesus valued me and offered me life," she continues, "I couldn't contain myself. I told everyone in town. I went from door to door. I even told the women who hated me. I didn't care. Everyone needed what Jesus had to offer, and I knew it. Before long they knew it too. Usually we Samaritans stayed away from the Jews, and the Jews avoided us. But Jesus stayed with us for two days. He and His disciples helped us to understand God and His love for us. And what He taught us, I need to tell you."

"It Doesn't Matter Where You Are—Jesus Values You"

"In my day Jews didn't go to Samaria. When Jews from Galilee went to Jerusalem for Passover, they used to cross over the Jordan River and go miles out of their way to avoid us. But Jesus didn't do that. He went where others did not want to go and did what others did not want to do—all for me. He will do the same for you. There is no place in this world that is too far or too alien or too difficult for God. He will go to the ends of the earth for you."

"It Doesn't Matter What You've Done—Jesus Values You"

"I've already told you that I was an outcast. Everyone in society shunned me, and the man I lived with in Sychar wasn't even kind to me. They were ashamed of me. And I was ashamed of myself. I had done things that anyone would hate to admit. But Jesus didn't care! He cared about me more than about my choices. He told me He came for people like me. And He came for people like you. There's nothing you could do to keep Jesus's love from you."

"It Doesn't Matter What You Believe—Jesus Values You"

"Perhaps the most surprising thing of all is that Jesus values you, no matter what you believe. During the two days Jesus was in the village, many people recognized that He was the Messiah, and they accepted His love and forgiveness. But many did not. Many rejected Him and insulted Him. He valued and loved them still.

"At the time I did not understand it. But now I do. God's love for us cannot be broken. It cannot be undone. We can reject it, but that doesn't stop Him from extending it to us. He values us no matter what."

The Prayer of the Samaritan Woman

The message she has for us is so simple. Yet it is the most important message in the history of humanity. God loves us, and He did go out of His way for us by sending Jesus to us. God has put heaven in our hearts. We just need to be willing to accept His gift of love.

"It is time for you to go," says the Samaritan Woman. "But first I want to pray for you.

> *"O Heavenly Father Who Loves Us,*
>
> *"It is astounding that You love us as You do. We are unworthy, yet You offer us Your love just the same. I ask that You help my friends here to sense Your love when they feel unlovable, and to be reassured. And out of that gift, may they share Your love with others. Amen.*

"If you continue on along this road, you will see a bridge. Cross over it. Your journey will end there. May God bless you."

Leadership Lessons

We follow her directions and walk farther down the road. I can't help thinking about how many people came to know Jesus because of her. How many in her village? How many who have read her story and realized it is also their story?

In a traditional sense, the Samaritan Woman was not a leader. She had no position or title. We don't even know what her name was. But she was an influencer, and that means she was a leader. Others followed her—right into heaven.

What can we learn from her?

1. Good Leaders Value People

No person can be a good leader and not care about others. People who don't care about others may be able to gather power. They may be able to manipulate people. But they cannot truly lead others unless they value them. No one modeled this better than Jesus did with the Samaritan Woman.

If you have responsibility for leading people, and you don't value them as individuals, then ask God to help you. I have found that when I haven't cared enough for others and I've asked God to help, He has softened my heart and rekindled my desire to love people.

2. Good Leaders Add Value to People

When you value people, you want to add value to them. Jesus did this every day with everyone. He was willing to help everyone who was willing to ask. And His spirit rubbed off on the Samaritan Woman. She tried to connect with everyone else in her village, because she saw that Jesus could change their lives for the better too.

Leaders are in a great position to help others. Every person you lead is a candidate for your ability to make them better, not just professionally, but personally. Everyone has a deep need to be loved, helped, and appreciated. You can become the kind of leader who brings value to people in these ways.

3. Good Leaders Don't Wait to Take Action

When the Samaritan Woman realized what was happening to her, she didn't wait around. She got moving. In fact, she left the well so quickly that she forgot her jar. She leaped into action. She wanted to do whatever she could to help people.

This is also the way Jesus operated. He took action. The fact that He spoke to the Samaritan Woman when it was considered taboo shows that He valued the right action over convention. Jesus was so rewarded by the outcome that He compared it to being fed. Jesus told His disciples,

> The food that keeps me going is that I do the will of the One who sent me, finishing the work he started. As you look around right now, wouldn't you say that in about four months it will be time to harvest? Well, I'm telling you to open your eyes and take a good look at what's right in front of you. These Samaritan fields are ripe. It's harvest time![35]

Jesus was exhorting His leaders to act. He wanted them to communicate the Gospel to others, and start leading them. He knew that the sooner they moved forward, the sooner they could help others and the more people they could help. Jesus still asks His leaders to do this even today.

The Samaritan Woman's fierce faith in God's love inspires me. Whatever fatigue I felt from climbing up the steep pathway at the cliff is now gone. If God is willing to go out of His way for me, then I'm willing to go out of my way for Him. I feel like I'm ready for anything, and I hope you are too.

Woman to Woman

The first time I heard the story of the Samaritan Woman, I was inspired by her experience with Jesus and how her life changed. The picture we envision of her leads to a painful past filled with disappointment, sadness, and loss of hope, causing a life full of low self-esteem. It was so low, in fact, that she hid from everyone. She was judged and hated by every woman in the village. She in turn felt extremely unloved and became very lonely. She looked for love and acceptance in all the wrong places.

Everything changed when she came face-to-face with Jesus. Jesus showed her something that nobody ever had before. He proved His unconditional love and mercy for her by talking with her and making her feel as though they had known each other forever. She became so excited and on fire for Him that she forgot her water jug by the well and ran through town telling everyone about the Messiah and His love for them, despite how they felt about her.

As women, we want to be loved and accepted. We want to be "wanted." Jesus gave her that love and acceptance. She overcame her innermost struggles through His unconditional love and turned them into a joy, which she wanted to spread to others. It made her bold and full of courage because she had faith in His ultimate love for her.

What I take away from this story is to never doubt Jesus, even when times are tough and I don't think I can go on. Jesus extends His grace and forgiveness to me unconditionally, no matter what I've done or how horrible I may feel about myself. He simply loves me.

The Samaritan Woman offered Jesus water to drink from the well, and in return He offered her living water, eternal life. We need to realize that Jesus doesn't care where we have been. He just wants us to end up loving Him, living for Him, and helping others to live for Him too. All we have to do is open up our hearts and let Him in.

—Maddie Miller

Questions for Reflection or Discussion

To learn more about the Samaritan Woman, read John 4:1–42.

1. In what ways, if any, do you identify with the Samaritan Woman?

2. Do you find it easy or difficult to believe that God loves you no matter what you've done or where you've been? Why?

3. Have there already been instances in your life where you sensed that God was going out of His way for you? If so, explain.

4. If you have not sensed that already, in what way would you *want* God to go out of His way for you?

5. What is your response to Jesus's claim that He was the Messiah and is the Son of God?

6. How do you feel about talking to others about Jesus Christ? Does it make you uncomfortable, or do you feel compelled to share your faith as the Samaritan Woman did? Why?

7. What is your greatest obstacle to taking on a leadership role? What could you do to overcome that obstacle?

CONCLUSION

We have walked only about a hundred yards when the road bends around a corner and we see the bridge. It's almost like a jetty. It leads to a small island not far from the shore. We walk across the bridge and arrive at a small pavilion.

Seated on a bench inside is my mother. She said I would see her again.

"Mom!" I say, and I grab her in a hug once more. I can't describe how I've missed her hugs.

"It's so good to see you again, Son," she says.

"Mom, the women we met were incredible. They really are giants of the faith. Let me tell you what we learned:

"Ruth taught us to follow our heart to find our hope.
"Sarah said we shouldn't complicate God's promise with our solution.

"Rahab told us that God's story is full of surprises.

"Hannah explained that God blesses the promises we keep to Him.

"Abigail said that a single act of wisdom can change our destiny.

"Miriam told us that comparison with others can rob us of our joy.

"Mary exhorted us not to miss our moment with God.

"Martha taught that when Jesus is in the house, we should give Him our full attention.

"The Samaritan Woman said that God will always go out of His way for us."

"I'm so glad, John," Mom says. "So it's been a good visit."

"It's been fantastic," I tell her, "but as much as I enjoyed it, I'd rather just sit and talk with you."

"I'm sorry, John. I wish you could stay longer, but your time here is done."

"Can't we talk, just for a little while?" I ask as we sit down next to her.

"That's not why you're here," says Mom with a smile. "But don't be sad. You and I will have an eternity to talk when the time comes." Mom grabs my hands, and the last thing I hear her say is, "Give my love to Margaret, my grandchildren, and my great-grandchildren."

I barely hear the last words because as she finishes them, my head begins to swim.

The next thing I know, I'm in my study sitting in my favorite thinking chair. *How long have I been gone?* I wonder. It's still dark outside. I look and see that the clock says it's 5:00 a.m.—the same time as when I closed my eyes.

Speaking of God, Scripture says, "A thousand years in your sight are like a day that has just gone by, or like a watch in the night."[36] Has God done all this in the blink of an eye? Or has this been a dream? The prophet Joel did say old men would dream dreams.[37] Either way, I've learned a lot, and God has given us a lot to think about.

NOTES

1. John 1:12.

2. Deuteronomy 24:19–22.

3. Deuteronomy 25:5–10.

4. Ruth 2:11–12, MSG.

5. Ruth 4:11–12, MSG.

6. 1 Peter 5:7, GNT.

7. Genesis 16:5, MSG.

8. Hebrews 11:31.

9. Matthew 1:15.

10. 1 Samuel 2:1, MSG.

11. 1 Samuel 2:10, MSG.

12. Judges 17:6, MSG.

13. 1 Samuel 3:19–21, MSG.

14. 1 Samuel 1:23, MSG.

15. 1 Samuel 25:10–11, MSG.

16. 1 Samuel 25:18–19, MSG.

17. 1 Samuel 25:23–25, MSG.

18. Psalm 31:23, NIV.

19. 1 Samuel 25:28–31, MSG.

20. 1 Samuel 25:31, MSG.

21. 1 Samuel 25:39–40, MSG.

22. James 1:5, NIV.

23. 1 Samuel 25:22, MSG.

24. Numbers 12:6–8, MSG.

25. Numbers 11: 28–29, MSG.

26. Luke 1:28, MSG.

27. Luke 1:31, MSG.

28. Luke 1:38, MSG.

29. John 2:5, MSG.

30. Luke 2:19.

31. John 11:21–22, MSG.

32. Luke 10:40, MSG.

33. John 12:8, MSG.

34. Philippians 2:5–8, MSG.

35. John 4:34–35, MSG.

36. Psalm 90:4, NIV.

37. Joel 2:28.

Look for John C. Maxwell's bestselling book

RUNNING WITH THE GIANTS
**What the Old Testament Heroes Want You to
Know about Life and Leadership**

In the race of life—a contest of stamina, endurance, faith, and understanding—we are never alone. Others have run it before us. In John C. Maxwell's vision of humanity, the giants of faith are in the stands, urging us on, praying for us, and offering the wisdom of their experience. We need only listen for their voices and hear their stories to turn our modern-day challenges into victories.

From David to Abraham, Moses to Rebekah, John Maxwell puts you face-to-face with towering figures of the Old Testament and shares the lessons you can learn from them about life, leadership, and yourself.

LEARNING FROM THE GIANTS
Life and Leadership Lessons from the Giants
John C. Maxwell

John Maxwell spends time with more giants of faith from the Old Testament in LEARNING FROM THE GIANTS. What valuable wisdom can we find in the lives of Elijah, Elisha, Job, Jacob, Deborah, Isaiah, Jonah, Joshua, and Daniel? These individuals fought and won epic battles, served kings, and endured great hardships for God to emerge transformed through  His grace. While exploring their experiences, Maxwell shares the timeless lessons you can learn about leadership, yourself, and your relationship with God.

Available now in print, electronic, and audio formats
from FaithWords wherever books are sold.